Can Political Violence Ever Be Justified?

Political Theory Today

Janna Thompson, *Should Current Generations Make Reparation for Slavery?*

Christopher Bertram, *Do States Have the Right to Exclude Immigrants?*

Diana Coole, *Should We Control World Population?*

Christopher Finlay, *Is Just War Possible?*

George Klosko, *Why Should We Obey the Law?*

Emanuela Ceva & Michele Bocchiola, *Is Whistleblowing a Duty?*

Elizabeth Frazer & Kimberly Hutchings, *Can Political Violence Ever Be Justified?*

Elizabeth Frazer
Kimberly Hutchings

Can Political Violence Ever Be Justified?

polity

First published in 2019 by Polity Press

Reprinted 2022

Polity Press
65 Bridge Street
Cambridge CB2 1UR, UK

Polity Press
101 Station Landing
Suite 300
Medford, MA 02155, USA

ISBN-13: 978-1-5095-2920-9
ISBN-13: 978-1-5095-2921-6 (pb)

A catalogue record for this book is available from the British Library.

Typeset in 11 on 15 Sabon by Servis Filmsetting Ltd, Stockport, Cheshire
Printed and bound in Great Britain by TJ Books Limited, Padstow

For further information on Polity, visit our website: politybooks.com

Contents

Introduction: The Question of Political Violence 1
1 Violence and Justification 7
2 Simple Justifications of Simple Violence 25
3 Complicating Matters 53
4 The Meaning of Political Violence 72
5 Against the Justification of Political Violence 95
Conclusion: Political Violence Can Never Be Justified 116

Sources and Further Reading 122

Introduction: The Question of Political Violence

Consider the following scenarios:

A: X has knowledge of terrorist networks that have been involved in violent attacks on civilian populations. The government approves the torture of X in order to gain information that will prevent such attacks.

B: X is a member of an oppressed majority population that has failed to gain its independence from colonial rule through non-violent methods. X takes up arms against the colonial power.

C: X knows that the current economic structure sustains massive exploitation, violence and oppression. X becomes committed to the overthrow of capitalism by all means necessary, including violence.

These decisions are simplified versions of actual events. All are also the subject of critical scrutiny by activists and scholars. Political violence is never a taken-for-granted political event; it always raises questions. Who has the right to authorize, or to use, violence? Against whom is it right to use it? What is the right way to use it? What limits should be placed on violence? All these questions are about what makes violence in politics justifiable. In this book, we address and respond to that issue in relation to different types and contexts of political violence, and draw on a range of cases and examples, including instances of these three scenarios: violence by states for the defence of populations and the maintenance of order; violence by non-state actors against colonial states, for liberation; and revolutionary violence by those seeking to transform the global political and economic order. We argue that the ways in which political violence has been justified now and in the past fail, and that political violence can never be justified.

Outline of the book

In chapter 1, we look more closely at our two key concepts: *political violence* and *justification*. We examine how political violence can be understood in narrower or broader terms, and what this implies for what counts as political violence, and therefore needs justification. We then analyse what justification means. We suggest that it means making an action *right*, prospectively. A level of confidence is needed, in advance, that the harms involved in political violence may be somehow compensated for or cancelled out by other considerations, such as good outcomes, laudable goals or some characteristic of the violence itself, perhaps the courage or unselfishness of the violent actor.

In chapter 2 we analyse justificatory arguments based on the idea that violence is one means to certain ends, using the examples of the campaigns of the Red Brigades in Italy and the Irish Republican Army (IRA) in Ireland in the 1970s, and of historic and contemporary anti-state, revolutionary violence. Consequentialists argue that certain ends (freedom, equality etc.) can justify the use of violent means. But pure consequentialist reasoning runs into difficulties; so some thinkers focus, in addition, on our rights, and what is permitted in defence of them; or on our duties, and whether violent action is either permissible or required in doing our duty. The thinkers we discuss tend to the view that whereas the violence of the state is to be taken for granted and needs no justification, the violence of people against established governments does need special justification. These thinkers also treat political violence in instrumental terms. Justifiable political violence is used to do something good.

Chapter 3 examines arguments that start from scepticism about the calculative tenor of that reasoning, drawing on perspectives influenced by marxism and existentialism, in the contexts of the stalinist purges of the 1930s, the nazi occupation of France in World War II and the anti-colonial struggle in Algeria in the 1950s and 1960s. From these perspectives, politics is not a realm in which means stand in stable relation to ends or in which violence is one option for political action amongst others. We examine analyses which emphasize the necessity, but also the unpredictable effects, of violence in politics, and go on to explore a range of alternative justifications of political violence, drawing on virtue and aesthetic categories.

Chapter 4 returns to issues about the meaning and scope of political violence. It raises problems for predominant conceptions, by introducing new arguments about structural and symbolic violence, and the nature of violence as a practice. Whereas thinkers in chapter 2 conceive of political violence as a specific episode or set of actions, the idea of structural violence locates political violence in social systems of material and ideological hierarchy, such as class, colonialism, racism or patriarchy. The discussion is further complicated by the work of Hannah Arendt, who argues that ideas in chapters 2 and 3 about justifying political violence rest on a misconception about the nature of politics. This, she argues, is antithetical to means-and-ends reasoning and cannot possibly provide justifications for the use of violence as a political means. In the final section, we consider how thinking about violence itself as a set of practices, for example the practice of torture or the practice of war, further complicates the idea that violence is a straightforward political tool, and draws attention to the kinds of political relations and values that inhere in violent actions and their conditions of possibility.

In chapter 5, drawing on material discussed in previous chapters, we return to arguments about particular instances of political violence – state use of interrogational torture against suspected terrorists, anti-colonial and anti-capitalist violence – and critique attempts to justify political violence. We argue that none of the justifications we have examined is persuasive, and moreover that these different justifications play a constitutive role in the practice of political violence. In our Conclusion we elaborate on our claim that political violence is never justified, and discuss its political implications.

1

Violence and Justification

Introduction

To address the question of whether political violence can be justified, we need to establish what we mean by political violence, and what counts as justification. This chapter sets out some preliminary thoughts.

Politics and violence

The term 'political violence' usually conjures up pictures of people rioting, damaging property, or visiting physical violence on each other in the context of political events and processes, for explicitly political purposes. It often involves police and security personnel whose job is to protect the existing social and political order, including policing demonstrations and counter-demonstrations. Protests around the world against economic-cultural globalization, against the treatment of landless people, against environmentally damaging public policies, and against unjust economic and fiscal regimes have sometimes turned into battles with the security personnel protecting conferences and meetings of the World Trade Organization, the World Bank and others. During violence after the disputed Kenyan elections in 2007, police shot violent demonstrators, in front of TV cameras, with the predictable effect that more violence was generated.

At least as frequent as this picture of rioters and protestors engaging with state officers are clashes between demonstrators and counter-demonstrators, campaigners and counter-campaigners. Counter-campaigners use physical threat or attack – from low-level breaking of cameras, or shouting down a speaker, to setting fire to or bombing rival organizations' offices. Equally frequent are cases of established governments or influential people within them using the institutions and forces of the state to attempt to suppress opposition – arresting opposition leaders and activists, for example as opposition leader Alexei Navalny has been imprisoned in Russia, or as Catalan political leaders have been arrested and charged, by the Spanish government and judiciary, for holding an unconstitutional referendum on national independence. In Zimbabwe, during the presidency of Robert Mugabe, there were many reports of intimidation of opposition activists by members of the ruling party.

Some readers might think that these examples muddle up political violence proper with state violence. Some thinkers, indeed, reserve the former category for the violence of citizens and denizens against an established state and government. In the chapters that follow we discuss reasons why thinkers and philosophers have made this distinction, between the political-legal 'force' reserved to and deployed by states, and the illegal (although perhaps morally justified) 'violence' that is used by citizens, denizens, aliens and other people who are members of the polity. Clearly, this is a difficult distinction to sustain.

First, the distinction 'state' and 'non-state' is too simple to capture the range of positions of the various members of a polity: those who exercise sovereign power and authority; police and security forces; civil servants; agents of the state who contract with governments to deliver public services; citizens (i.e. those who have the full set of rights to a passport, to vote, to stand for office); denizens (i.e. those who live on the territory of a state but are not citizens); aliens (visitors, illegal denizens); members of parties competing for office and governmental power; members of campaigning groups trying to put pressure on, or to oppose, government; members of cultures which are positioned in opposition to the dominant cultural groups, or don't participate in public life. There are others. In the theory of popular sovereignty and democracy some of these people, but not all, constitute 'the state' – although which do varies from theory to theory. In law, some are deemed to be citizens and others not, and these various classes of person are accorded various rights and obligations. But these laws are always politically contested. In popular political culture some are outsiders and some insiders. Again, the distinction is invariably contested.

Second, from the point of view of political science, 'core state' institutions, including the executive (and the 'core executive'), the judiciary, the police, the military and the legislature, are clearly 'state' institutions. But there is a continuum of state power, through corporations and agents contracted to the state for the supply of goods and services including security, through the political parties that contend for state power, to schools, cultural organizations and other institutions that discharge 'state' functions like education and health, and rely on state resources for their survival. Violence occurs in and around all of these institutions, sometimes, and some of it is political violence in the sense that it has political functions, is for political purposes, has political effects, or takes place in the midst of explicitly political processes like elections, or contestations over policy, or revolutions.

Third, the arrest and imprisonment of opposition figures must clearly count as political violence – it is for explicitly political purposes. But is this 'state' violence? Or is it the violence of governmental actors taking advantage of their control of state resources for their personal or partisan political purposes?

Fourth, there are hazy and contested distinctions between 'political' and other forms of violence. Personal, and local, antagonisms are very likely to get muddled up with political issues at times of contention. In civil wars, it is difficult to say what the causes and explanations of patterns of antagonism are, because people's position in the war can be to take the opposite side from that of those who are already their enemies. 'Political violence' is often mixed up with inter-communal violence – especially, but not only, where party loyalty follows ethnic, or religious, or clan or other communal identification and membership. In cases of riot, or electoral violence, criminal gangs can take the opportunity to get involved, for the sake of theft, or for territorial purposes. The fact that police and government spokespersons, especially in broadly liberal democratic polities, associate political demonstrators with 'criminals' as a way of delegitimizing the political action, and use criminal law for the purposes of prosecution, only intensifies this contested relationship between crime and politics.

Given the vagueness of these distinctions, between institutions, actors and kinds of violence, a more plausible approach might be to include in the category of political violence all violence connected to political purposes broadly conceived, including winning, securing, stabilizing, destabilizing, deploying and challenging power. President Putin's treating political opposition as criminal is a political use of violence, just as surely as is the physically intimidatory shouting down of a campaigner for a controversial position in a dispute over an issue like abortion, or sex and gender identity. The justificatory work these actions might involve is likely to vary: a president will talk of state security, and the sovereign deployment of legal force, where a protestor will talk of constitutional rights, governmental accountability, moral rights, popular sovereignty or freedom of speech. We should not, either, confine matters of politics to affairs of state. Changes in society, or in culture, when pursued or argued about publicly, are political. They rely on legislation and protection for particular positions. Some positions that today are illegal might be legalized in future, and vice versa. That's the point of a good deal of politics. There's more to it than legalization or illegalization, however. Political power – the power to influence, to get things done, to persuade, to organize, to win the authority to rule (or to lose it) – is not exhausted by law. Violence that asserts, expresses or enforces the denigration or subjugation of others on grounds of race, nationality, sexuality or gender is political, since it is about the preservation of power privilege, whether carried out by state or private actors.

Thinking about political violence also raises the question of what counts as violence. The distinction between state 'force' and other violence identifies political violence with what is illegal, or unjustified. The concept of violence, when applied to human affairs, always involves an idea of 'violation' of a norm, but that does not amount to illegality or illegitimacy. For example, there is a norm against punching someone on the jaw. On the face of it this is criminal assault. But the norm is overridden in the context of boxing practice or competition. The boxer uses a degree of force that overcomes the resistance of the opponent; the action is so speedy that the opponent can't evade the punch; the blow hurts, or even injures. Boxing is violent, but it is a regulated, legal violence. There is a norm against using a chemical like CS gas to incapacitate a person. That too is on the face of it a criminal act. But the norm is overridden when tear gas is used, in accordance with law and authority, by police officers against protestors. We do not say that boxing, or uses of CS gas in crowd control, are not violent. Rather, they are legal violence. Nor does this imply that they are justified. In both cases, there are principled objections to the relevant laws. Some argue, coherently, that fist fighting should not be elevated to the sport of boxing, precisely because the underlying violence and risk of the engagement make it morally different to other athletic contests. Some argue that police officers should not be allowed to use tear gas, water cannon or Tasers against protestors. Although, in some countries, these policing techniques are legal, that does not in itself justify them.

So far we have focused on instances of physical assault and threats of physical violence. During the anti-globalization protests in Seattle in 1999 the shop windows of global brands were broken; police used weapons, and enforced routes for protestors, and confined them in certain areas; protestors threw stones and other missiles at police. In Kenya there were deadly attacks and deliberate killings of rival party members and individuals from particular ethnic groups. In Russia and Spain leaders of opposition political parties and movements have been arrested and imprisoned, on charges ranging from treason to public disorder.

Some critics are concerned that focus on killing, imprisonment, destruction of property and physical injury misses a whole dimension of violence, which is very effective, and very injurious, but does not confine persons as imprisonment does, or leave scars on the body. These critics argue that in order to understand the relative severity of instances and patterns of violence, we have to take into account the structural and symbolic violence of states, the global system of capitalism, white and masculine privilege as much as the physical injury and trauma that are visited on people by them. You don't have to actually hit a poor person to injure them or shorten their life: that is already done by depriving them of the goods needed for flourishing, like clean water. You don't often have to kettle a citizen on a demonstration, or hit them with tear gas, in order to quell opposition to the dominant political and economic order. That is already done by narrowing down people's options and values to the point where they only want what global capitalists are willing to sell them, and don't value political participation for themselves. You don't often have to physically attack young black men if none of them has the economic opportunity to live in your neighbourhood. You don't often have to actually beat a woman as long as she is already persuaded of her inferiority and incapacity to make decisions. These, according to critics, are material and ideological processes that are as violent as the truncheons or water cannon of the security services, the shooting and incarceration of black men, or the killing of women in domestic settings. They are also processes that enable and support such direct violence. The imprisonment of opposition leaders, on this account, is only the tiniest tip of a massive iceberg of state- and status-quo-preserving violence, most of which is perpetrated silently, without leaving visible scars, but which oppresses, represses and damages. If we are to ask whether it can be justified for a campaigner to set a bomb, or a protestor to throw stones at security personnel, we might also consider how, if at all, this more widespread violence might be justified.

Justification

What is it to justify an action or course of action? When we think about something being justified or justifiable, we think of it as in some sense being made right. One influential way of thinking about this is that an action, or a circumstance, system or rule, is justified if its consequences or outcomes are good. There are various and rival ways of formulating this. An act of violence might be justified because it brings about good and eliminates evil. The apparently negative qualities of the violence are outweighed by the positive value of the consequences, on a cost–benefit analysis. Violence is the price of a good. Or (bad) violence is a means to the (good) outcome or end. In this means–ends frame violence is an instrument that might be used to achieve certain ends. It's a dangerous instrument, to be sure, but for particular ends the risks and the damaging side effects involved are worth it. The ends, or goals, obviously, have to be very good and desirable – justice, equality, the defeat of evil – before we can consider using a bad like violence as means. Racist or ethnically discriminatory attacks and killings in order to establish ethnic political dominance in a polity and society cannot be justified by their ends, which are permanent discrimination and exclusion, the establishment of inequality. Using violence when an electoral process is going against you, in order to gain or maintain governing power, is not justified. But when an unjust government or international governance organization fails to adopt policies and processes that deliver justice, when the normal political processes that should be oriented to the securing of justice for all fail, then it may be justified to turn to violent means.

A problem, obviously, for this line of reasoning is the contestation of the concept of justice or good which is the required end or aim for a justified violent action. All kinds of political actors – authoritarians, fascists, racists and capitalists, as well as socialists, libertarians, feminists and cosmopolitans – claim justice as their goal. They have radically divergent understandings of what is just: for some it is established hierarchy and oppression of the 'inferior', for others it is equality and the satisfaction of all persons' basic needs. For some it is whatever emerges from individual choice and free contract; for others it is an equalized, or unequal, distribution of goods and burdens that requires continual social, political and legal action to achieve and maintain.

Consequentialist reasoning poses further problems. Obviously, the outcomes of a course of action can't be known in advance. They can be calculated, given what we know about causes and effects in normal circumstances. We can estimate the probabilities of things working out according to the plan. But of course things can go wrong, and the expected (or hoped-for) consequences might not transpire. Things are complicated when the short-term consequences of a political intervention are bad, or very costly, but might nevertheless be weighed against medium- or long-term good or better consequences. Here there is a corresponding diminution in certainty regarding what the actual outcomes will be.

Because of such difficulties with consequentialism, broadly speaking, many thinkers and activists have recourse to other kinds of moral justification. One way is to move the burden of justification from actual consequences and shift focus instead to the actor's goals or aims, or the intentions of the agent. There is still some indeterminacy, of course, as what agents say they intend might vary from their true motivation. But on the whole, having good intentions but bringing about harm is better, morally (and, often, legally) speaking, than bringing about harm with ill intentions. Similarly, doing good by luck or by accident has a different moral quality from doing good intentionally, out of virtue. Another way is to take issue with the moral priority of 'consequences', or 'overall consequences'. The problem is that acting to bring about the best consequences can, in theory, be at the expense of the right and the good of some. Familiarly, we might calculate that it is better for an agent to kill or harm one individual if the alternative is that a larger number – ten, or a hundred – of individuals be killed or harmed. Is it better, or acceptable, to bring about a benefit to ten, or a thousand, at the expense of the life of or great harm to one? Of course, our intuitions vary, both with the numbers, and with the detail of the story of how and why benefit and harm are to be distributed. But for many thinkers, the right to life, or the basic human rights, of any one individual should outweigh the good consequences overall of harming them so that some number of other people can benefit. That is, we can't just weigh up the consequences of violence. We have to give special weight to rights in deciding whether or not it is justified.

Rights theory by no means always tells against violence, though. Depending on circumstances, that individuals enjoy human rights can mean that people have the right, and even the duty, to use violence – for instance, in order to defend innocent victims' human rights. Just as consequentialist reasoning can conclude that violence for justice is justified by good (egalitarian, just) consequences, or because it was engaged in with the explicit intention of bringing about justice, so rights theory can conclude that violence is justified because some people's rights make it permissible, or even that agents have an obligation to use violence in defence of their or other people's rights.

Another type of justification refers, rather, to the idea of necessity. As political agents, we are not calculators, estimating the probabilities of achieving our aims, and weighing them against the costs and risks of our tactical means. We don't reason about who has what rights or obligations to do what. Rather, we are in a violent situation, and there is no choice about engaging with it. The point here is that established power structures of capital, exploitation and oppression, of social hierarchies like racism, patriarchy or hierocracy, themselves rely on violence for their maintenance. We know that violence is deployed, in defence of the status quo, against those who challenge it. Women who challenge established sexual hierarchy know what the cost of energetic opposition is. Anyone who tries to take on capitalism and its inequalities knows what states and corporations do in order to quell opposition. In such settings, violence is not one means of political change among many which might be chosen. Engaging with violence which is non-optional must mean either engaging in violence, or allowing the violence of the dominant to have its way.

Political agents who accept this theory still have to answer the charge that responding to violence with violence is to meet evil with evil, which is an unwinnable contest. So thinkers have articulated ways of distinguishing between their violence and others', or good versus bad violence. In doing this they often invoke virtue or aesthetic criteria, or draw analogies between the practice of revolutionary violence and other characteristics or situations. The violence of the oppressors is characterized as brutal, cowardly and ugly, the work of people who hide behind overwhelming technological force. The violence of the radicals, the revolutionaries, is heroic, clean and beautiful. In the history of political thought, the idea that the oppressors are effeminate, while the revolutionaries are manly, is frequently expressed.

Distinctions between good and bad, right and wrong, virtuous and vicious, ugly and beautiful violences, as well as being based on principles such as consequentialism, rights and duties, or necessity, also trade a good deal on analogies. For many thinkers and activists, engagement in political violence is like self-defence. For some, engaging in political violence is like rescue: just as a civil officer who rescues a victim from a car crash, or from a burning building, might have to hurt, even injure, the victim in the course of rescue, so some violence to a society, or a social group, might be justified in the course of liberation from oppression. In the history of political thinking, a great deal of justificatory work has been done by drawing an analogy between political action and war. All such analogies condition in particular ways how political action is thought of – political actors are civil heroes, or warriors.

In what follows we consider the implications of these and other justificatory analogies and arguments. We attempt always to be clear about the inevitable ambiguity of the term 'justification'. It refers both to the process or practice of justifying, and to the product of that process. A justification in the latter sense is a logical argument which justifies; the validity of such arguments is always in question.

Conclusion

All the concepts that are key to the argument of this book are subject to contestation. People disagree about what counts as *political* in political violence, for example excluding legal actions from the category, or identifying *political* exclusively with non-state. People disagree about the meaning of *violence*, and whether the category should or should not include systemic conditions, such as racism or sexism. And people disagree about what counts as *justification*. In what follows, we encounter these contestations again, and see how different understandings of the meanings of both politics and violence condition the possibilities for what might count as justification. We will begin by examining the most prevalent arguments for the justification of political violence, starting with consequentialist arguments.

2

Simple Justifications of Simple Violence

Introduction

Here we focus on some of the most familiar ways in which political violence has been justified. We look first at consequentialist arguments, and then at how they have been modified and challenged by reference to actors' intentions, or the overriding value of certain rights, in particular the right to self-defence or defence against unjust attack. We show that these justificatory arguments rely on certain assumptions about the relationship between means and ends, and on an understanding of political violence as an act or series of acts carried out by individual agents.

Consequences

In the 1970s, in Europe and North America, a particular form of political violence, with a particular justification, was deployed to challenge established forms of government, authority and power.

In Italy, fascist groups, convinced that marxism and communism posed a continued threat to state, society and church, organized intimidation and violence against unions and left political organizations. Left-wing groups organized to oppose what their members saw as the heritage of fascism and nazism. They were also critical of soviet communism, and concerned to reclaim a marxism and left politics that was distinct from the soviet-influenced communist parties, from the 'euro-communism' that developed in western Europe, and also from the social democratic parties that were sharing governmental power in western European countries. Networks, groups and projects to defend working-class interests in cities and workplaces were established. Some of these autonomous left organizations developed the view that violence was not only necessary in defence against fascist attack, but also, if directed at institutions of state and economy, could weaken those institutions, and encourage widespread, effective revolutionary action and transformation of structure and system.

From 1969 to the mid-1970s there were numerous violent attacks in Italy. Right-wing attacks outnumbered left ones by ten to one and included bombings and beatings. The incidence of fascist attacks diminished in the second half of the 1970s, as support for them in the parliamentary Christian Democratic Party was withdrawn. There were some left-wing attacks on right-wing groups, but the autonomous left mainly embarked on a campaign of sabotage, attacks on vehicles, and kidnaps of notable industrial and political figures. The most notorious left attack was the kidnapping and murder of Prime Minister Aldo Moro in 1978, carried out by the Red Brigades. The Red Brigades were untypical organizationally, consisting of small closed cells, rather than the more common cooperative network with local presence and arm's-length affiliations to more tightly organized violent groups. Over the whole of the 1970s, the Red Brigades were responsible for 25 per cent of left-wing attacks.

In Northern Ireland decades of systematic social, economic and political exclusion of catholic people, many of whom were politically in favour of reunification with Eire, and also favoured redistributive welfare state programmes, so in political terms were left wing, generated an increasingly energetic and engaged protest movement which staged demonstrations in support of civil rights for catholics – effective voting and representation rights, and also fairness in housing, employment and education. The civil rights movement became prominent in October 1968 when the Northern Ireland police attacked a demonstration with baton charges. As in Italy, some fractions of the civil rights movement became committed to explicit uses of organized violence, against the police, against the dominating protestant community in general and, later, against the British Army which was deployed to 'keep the peace'. Eventually the provisional Irish Republican Army (IRA), which had its roots in the nineteenth- and early twentieth-century Irish nationalist and independence conflicts with the British state, embarked on a campaign of violent attacks on the British mainland. During the 1970s numerous bombings against British targets were carried out, the vast majority by the IRA, although there were some attacks by protestant militant organizations against locations associated with catholic residents or with IRA sympathies.

Governmental, news media and popular social response mainly focused on the outrageous nature of the attacks, the loss of innocent lives, health or property, and the commitment of the polity, economy and society to the principle of not giving in to violence. In response, those sympathetic to the aims of the Irish republicans and catholics pointed out the long history of violence against Irish people in general and catholics in particular that had been prosecuted by the British state, which, for many critics, was a colonialist occupying state as it was elsewhere in the world. In other words, it was noted that there is a kind of hypocrisy in condemning violent acts by protesters and would-be revolutionaries while condoning exactly similar, but markedly more extensive, acts by the officers of the dominant state. These critics also pointed out the hypocrisy in the disproportionate rage engendered by attacks on the British mainland, as opposed to those on the island of Ireland. Such concerns raise vividly the question of what political violence can be justified and how.

Among the philosophical works considering the question of the justification of this kind of political violence, Ted Honderich's *Three Essays on Political Violence* (first published 1977) are notable. For our purposes they can be taken as representative of a very influential consequentialist form of justificatory argument. They were framed specifically in the context of the 1970s conflicts, as a response to knee-jerk condemnations of violence, appealing to the equally intuitive thought that some acts of violence are clearly justified by their consequences. An obvious candidate is the German resistance's attempted assassination of Hitler in 1944. The perpetrators judged that the removal of that one person from the regime would make a material difference to the subsequent course of the world war and the future of Germany. If successful, the action would clearly have been justified by the fact that the benefits of its outcomes outweighed its costs.

This kind of consequentialist thinking raises a number of difficulties. There is a difference between the justification of an action in advance of its being perpetrated (ex ante), and the subsequent perception of the act as having had good consequences (ex post justification). The German resistance plotters had to take a forward-looking risk: they betted that the assassination had a reasonable chance of succeeding, and that the outcomes would be overall good, or, at least, less bad than the outcomes of not acting. Similarly, the IRA, the Red Brigades, the fascists and the protestant groups all judged that their violence would open up opportunities for political transformation, with eventual outcomes better than the status quo.

This analysis, which puts the German resistance

to nazism on an equal footing with the Italian post-war fascists, raises an obvious objection. The revised edition of Honderich's essays (1980) was titled *Violence for Equality* – explicitly emphasizing the kinds of ends and consequences towards which violence is aimed. Rather than focusing on consequences as such, the analysis focuses on the actors' goals and intentions. Fascist gangs beating up Italian trades unionists are morally distinct from the left groups who sabotage a factory which discriminates against Northern Irish catholics. The demonstrators for civil rights caught up in the violence of heavy-handed armed policing are on the same side as those who use violence against state targets in pursuit of class justice. Having the correct aims and ends is necessary, although not sufficient, to justify violence. Honderich's essays introduce two further criteria.

First, violence can only be used in the last resort. It would not be necessary if governments did what they should to secure justice. Governmental power is best placed to bring equality about. The British and Northern Ireland governments could have ensured that the kind of discrimination against catholics that was ubiquitous in industries and occupations be made illegal, subject to punishment and widely condemned. They could have enforced civil rights

– effective rights to vote, to elect councillors, to participate in the governance of the polity. They did not. The Italian government could have insisted that justice for working people be at the heart of industrial policy. The Italian left disputed the dominant view that capitalist industrialization was the best way forward for Italy post war, and that the welfare and social institutions adequately addressed social deprivation. Such facts should make a salient difference to the decision making of protestors and campaigners for civil rights and social justice. If governments will not secure justice it is imperative that someone else act for equality. Groups with motivation, organization and resources at their disposal are positioned to act, and, on the face of it, have an agent prerogative, a kind of right, to do so. Their action, for equality, then might be justified.

Only 'might', because, second, what they do must be judged to have a reasonable chance of success. The German resistance judged their planned action to have a good chance of killing Hitler, and they also judged that had Hitler died there was a reasonable chance that remaining members of the regime would have been more amenable to ceasing the exterminations and ending the war. The judgement of probabilities has to be accompanied by a reasonable theory of what the mechanisms of the desired change will be. For the Red Brigades and the IRA, the question is how sabotaging factories, bombing symbolically important governmental or economic sites, or kidnapping for ransom key political or economic figures could bring about justice. Obviously, this isn't the same way that successfully assassinating Hitler might have, or the same way as securing governmental legislation by public political means such as campaigns for reform. The latter works, when it does, by persuading key actors that the change is either just and right or, at any rate, democratically legitimate and called for. The left violent groups judged that the government wouldn't do the right thing because it is right, or democratically called for. But, they judged, the government would weaken if threatened and intimidated. Relatedly, some judged that people who have been marginalized and excluded can come to greater social prominence, and gain greater democratic voice and ability to shape government, by an act of self-assertion like a use of violence.

Focus on the probability of success, and on the moral quality of the aims and objectives of violent actors, means, then, that consequentialist reasoning is not purely consequentialist. First, justification of an act – from the perspective of the perpetrators and their audiences – has to be in advance of the consequences, when the consequences can only be guessed at. The attempted assassination of Hitler was not successful. The immediate aftermath included terrible retributions and thousands of executions, including of the would-be assassins. Of course, this failure alone does not condemn the perpetrators of the act. Their bet on success can be judged to be sound, even though luck was not on their side. History has judged that their motivations were good, even though some of them had before been deeply involved in nazi atrocities. But this raises a second problem for consequentialism. Aims and motivations can't be certain. Critics of political violence often suspect that perpetrators do not have morally admirable ideals, but are engaged in violence for revenge, out of anger or resentment, or have some other somatic and emotional investment in violent action. Indeed, divisions of labour within political (and social) groups and movements, leaving violence to the violent, testify to complexity of motive and action. Similarly, our judgement that the Hitler assassination plotters were either acting out of morally admirable motives, or were admirably redeeming their past crimes, requires us, the judges, to take a view of their characters (and historians, since, have certainly studied the records and motives of the plotters). Honderich himself, though, explicitly rejects arguments that focus on the agent or the actor, asking whether she acted with integrity, or whether the quality of her character affects our judgement of her culpability or praiseworthiness. He emphasizes that it is consequences, or goals, alone that should be the points on our moral compass.

Critics have attacked Honderich's theory for its permissive view of violence. This was so in particular when he published a new revised version in 2003, with the title *Terrorism for Humanity*, in response to the Al Qaeda terrorist bombings on September 11, 2001. Such accusations are unjustified, given his argument. The requirements of justice in aims, and of a degree of certainty about success in achieving those aims, are actually very restrictive. However, the argument that violence – on the part of unjustly oppressed groups – works, and can be morally and politically justified by reference to its consequences, recurs in radical thinking and is denied by conservatives. In particular, anarchist activists in the context of the anti-capitalism actions that have developed since the late 1980s have focused on the effectiveness of violent protest. Developing out of environmental protest and direct action politics, and out of solidarity actions with landless people, an effectively global network of activists has coordinated demonstrations and direct actions especially targeted at international financial organizations such as the World Bank, the International Monetary Fund, and the meetings of states that have organized themselves as the 'groups': the Group of 6 founded in 1975, later developed into the G8 in 1997, subsequently with the suspension of Russia called the G7, and so on. Actions have attempted to derail meetings – beginning with the Berlin International Monetary Fund and World Bank meetings in 1988 – and to propel demands for debt cancellation or environmentally friendly policies, or against work conditions in global industries, on to the international political agenda. A number of these actions have been characterized by significant clashes between protestors and state and private security personnel – for example at the 1999 Seattle World Trade Organization conference.

There have been significant disagreements and tensions within the broad anti-globalization movement, between parties and groups with different aims or political programmes – for instance disagreements between activists with socialist, marxist, anarchist, environmentalist or feminist identifications and commitments. And there have been clashes between groups committed to non-violent actions and those who are committed rather to a 'diversity of tactics' – i.e. the permissibility and inclusion of violent actions.

According to those who advocate diversity of tactics, violent tactics are effective – and more effective, history shows, than pacifist and other non-violent strategies and tactics. An obvious objection is that the reasoning of political realists can just as well go the other way. A government that won't do the right thing for its own sake is also not likely to do the right thing because it faces violence. A society that marginalizes a particular group – the autonomous left, or a religious and cultural minority, as catholics were in Northern Ireland – is not likely to accord that group greater respect, or democratic voice and legitimacy, because they act violently. The plausibility of the argument for violent tactics seems to rest on the idea that unjust governments and societies are also cowardly. But equally plausible is that unjust governments and societies are also very violent themselves, deploying considerable police and military violence in support and defence of the status quo. So the likelihood of the violence of protesters and activists being successful might be judged to be diminished.

The actions of organizations like those involved in the Italian and Northern Ireland campaigns keep our focus where Honderich's was: on the 'considerable or destroying use of force against persons, things, or systems of government'. Whether the violent actions of groups like the Italian autonomous left, anti-globalization protestors or nationalist terrorists are justified is a question that seems both to be susceptible to the same kind of reasoning as, and to be different from, the questions of whether the violence of the Italian police, the Northern Ireland security forces, the forces protecting international agencies and events, or those seeking to prevent and punish terrorists is justified. Because of the complication of the distinction between the force of 'the state' and the violence of those who act against the state or contrary to the law, much ethical analysis focuses specifically on the possible violence of protestors and campaigners, and confines the category of political violence to non-state actors.

But the magnitude of the consequences of a decision to meet an instance of potential disorder with a violent security response, or to tolerate partiality for one party in a social and cultural contention – as fractions of the Italian police and government were implicated with fascist groups, or as the Northern Irish police were identified with the protestant cause – makes it difficult to see why our justificatory reasoning about 'violence for equality' should be any different from our reasoning about 'violence for social order'. In each case, according to the consequentialist philosophical strategy, we have to evaluate ends, means and causal probabilities.

Rights

One argument for making a clear distinction between the violence of organized political groups against each other and against the state, on the one hand, and the violence of police, government and security forces, on the other, is that the latter have within their prerogatives and constitutional authority the right to enforce law and to punish. Police violence against protesters, or against the perpetrators of bombings or kidnappings, is pursuant to state punishment. Arguably, this makes our reasoning about justifiability different in the two cases. However, this question of the right to punish takes us to a distinct tradition of justifying violence – one that is based on individuals' natural right to punish (rather than states' political right) and their natural right of self-defence. It justifies certain forms of violence by non-state actors, for instance 'violence for equality', in these terms, challenging the distinction that is accepted in the work of Honderich and others.

We begin this story in seventeenth-century Britain, with the English civil wars of 1642–51, the execution of Charles I in 1649, the eventual restoration of the monarchy under Charles II in 1660, and the succession crisis – concern that the throne might be inherited by a roman catholic – following James II's accession in 1685. In the end this culminated in the abdication, or the overthrowing, of James and the coronation of the protestant Queen Mary (James's elder daughter) and her husband William of Orange in 1688. All this is the context for the writing, and more importantly for the reception, of John Locke's *Two Treatises of Government*. The work can be, and has been, read as a defence of the events of 1688 – its publication in 1690 is certainly apropos – but historians agree that it was composed in the late 1670s or early 1680s. For Locke and his readers the memory of the execution of Charles I, and of the violent civil war that preceded it, was vivid. Locke's argument implies that, were Charles I properly deemed to have violated the sovereign trust, and to have endangered the state and the security of the people within it (which some of his enemies certainly argued that he had), then his violent end would be justified, so that the people could select a new sovereign and government of their choice.

Locke's idea of a state of nature – without government, sovereign power, laws or state punishments – allows him to think about risks and dangers we would face in such a state, and what rights we would have as natural, non-political beings. In Locke's construction, we would have natural rights to gather, hunt and labour in order to maintain subsistence and welfare for ourselves and our dependants, and rights to safety in our persons and security in our property. The natural law forbids assault, theft and murder. According to Locke, just as men naturally may use violence against wild beasts like polecats, so they may against human predators – people who attempt to steal our property or assault us. This violence has two aspects. It is, of course, self-defence. But when perpetrated by a person who lives by and respects the natural law, and in a state of nature, it further constitutes our natural punishment of those who violate the natural law.

In political societies, governed by lawful sovereignty – and where those who are governed by the laws have by implication consented to them – we give up our natural right to punish. Instead, we agree to obey the law ourselves, and that we or others who disobey it should be judged and punished by those with the relevant offices. The sovereign and legislature are entrusted with the power to make the laws; the magistrates direct the officers of the executive – the police, the prison authorities etc. – to punish us if we are guilty of crime. Critically, according to Locke, the sovereign herself or himself, and the magistrates, police and prison authorities, as well as the citizens, are all bound to obey the laws.

If the sovereign violates the sovereign trust, political power (which is based on this crucial agreement that we should all be bound by offices and laws) effectively ceases to operate. Everyone then is thrown back in to something like a state of nature, with their natural powers and rights. Just as, naturally, you have a right to defend yourself against a wild beast that attacks your person or your property and threatens your safety, so when the sovereign himself disobeys the law, and endangers the commonwealth, then we are justified in defending ourselves against him, and indeed punishing him. The way Locke uses the analogy of wild beasts (lions, polecats) throughout his argument, and the way he argues that when the sovereign himself violates the law the social compact is effectively destroyed and political power ceases, the way he uses the theme of self-defence and the natural right to punish those who violate the natural law – all conduce to our reading this argument as justifying, in the end, even violent means of overthrowing a sovereign.

Locke's arguments, in his time, were directed against two influential positions that denied the validity of his inference from a natural right to self-defence, or a natural right to punish, to the right to remove sovereign power, and to use violence in so doing. First was the very influential patriarchalist theory, according to which kings were descended from Adam, to whom God had given the authority to rule, over his descendants and over women. In this theory, rights belong to patriarchs, primarily, and by inheritance to men. Second, Thomas Hobbes, in *Leviathan* (1651), composed during the Commonwealth period after the execution of Charles I, had argued that the sovereign's authority should be deemed to be absolute. This is not because God had said so, but because given the alternative – a state of nature in which there is no law, no security, constant fear of assault and theft by stronger predatory individuals – the only reasonable step for men to take is to select a sovereign and give him absolute, unchallengeable authority. The alternative is that challenges to the existing sovereign's authority can degenerate into the kind of violent rivalry, polarization and deep disagreement that permits violence and repeated civil wars.

Locke straightforwardly disagrees with Hobbes about this threat of the 'war of all against all', insisting that in the state of nature people have the capacities for reasoning, bargaining, cooperating and, indeed, agreeing to set up rules and institutions. That is what explains political society to begin with. Locke also thinks that the contention of political power does not automatically mean war. That's the point of constitutions. Anyway, according the sovereign such absolute authority is likely to be conducive to abuse and violence by the sovereign. As Locke puts it, Hobbes seems to think that in order to get away from the threats of polecats or foxes, it is advisable to put oneself into the way of devouring lions.

More importantly for this book, however, Locke and Hobbes disagree about the nature of the violence that is, or is not, to be justified. Locke takes it that men naturally have the wherewithal for violence; and that some of them will have tendencies to violent action that endanger other people and endanger the society. That is, there is a context of natural and social violence. Naturally, violence may be used against the violent. In a political society we rely on laws, and on law enforcement agents, to defend us, and to punish anyone who assaults us. The government in political society, that is, is permitted to use violence where the rest of us are not. But equally, there can be situations in which we are permitted to participate in uses of violence, against the government. For Locke, violence against the state, for justice, might be justified.

Hobbes's argument is that all violence must be monopolized by the sovereign. This doesn't mean that only the sovereign uses violence. The sovereign will use 'the sword' to punish criminals or repress rebellions, but more importantly will get to say what other violence may be used by whom against whom, deploying the sceptre of sovereign legislative power. So parents might be permitted to physically punish their children, up to a point; boxers may be allowed to fight with fists, wearing gloves and in a licensed ring; some kinds of fights between individuals count as criminal and as assaults, while others might be permitted as play; and so on. This means that violence, being by permission of the sovereign, can or should never be used against the sovereign. Violence in society can only be permitted, or criminal, or treasonous. This also means effectively that there are no limits on the violence the sovereign can use against citizens.

Hobbes's theory can be and has been interpreted as supporting the claims of authoritarian leaders that they cannot be held to account for the nature of their rule, and that having once been selected as sovereign they cannot be removed. Locke opposes all these implications of Hobbes's theory: the absolute inadmissibility of violence against the sovereign or his forcible overthrow, its classification as treasonous, and the unlimited nature of sovereign rule. For Locke, the force against James II was not treason, and had a measure of violence been used against James, that would not have been treasonous either. This is because sovereignty lies with the people who make up the commonwealth or state, collectively. It is related to and derived from the sovereignty over self that they enjoy as natural beings.

We said that Locke was addressing two views opposed to his own – patriarchalism and absolutism. Subsequently to his own time, his rights theory has been opposed by a view that puts the moral duties that people have, under reason (as opposed to under nature), first. Immanuel Kant, in the *Grounding for the Metaphysics of Morals* (1785), finds that the duty not to harm others or to use them as a means to our own ends (in his formulation, the duty always to treat them as ends in themselves), is a perfect duty which strictly prohibits violence as well as killing. So the question of whether I can defend myself, if attacked, can look puzzling from a kantian perspective. Harming someone else because I do not wish to be harmed by them looks like a case of treating them as means to my own ends. This kind of imperative account of natural or moral law has been very influential in pacifism – in the work of Leo Tolstoy, who, for example in *The Kingdom of God is Within You* (1894), interprets christian (New Testament) ethics in terms of this kind of absolute prohibition on violence.

According to this line of thinking, the question of whether the German resistance actors were justified in their attempt to assassinate Hitler is answered clearly in the negative. The consequences overall of their action are irrelevant to our reasoning. The punishment of Hitler, had he lived to stand trial in a court of law, is a different matter for Kant. Punishment in the context of rule and law is clearly justifiable. However, this does not extend to anything like the 'people's right to punish', or to use violence in pursuit of political ends. Kant's political philosophy, then, raises puzzles about the justifiability of the French revolution – which he, personally, supported. Long-standing and deep-seated regime and state failure, demands for representative and parliamentary reforms, and urgent needs for poverty alleviation met intransigent statements of absolute authority from King Louis XVI throughout the 1780s. Developing pressure from parliamentary deputies, and developing social unrest, eventuated in the revolutionary events of 1789, among which the women's march to Versailles resulted in the king – under a good deal of physical pressure and threat – returning to Paris to acknowledge popular sovereignty and the authority of the assembly. In Kant's view the 1789 revolution realized the kind of individual freedom which is a necessary condition for rights and our capacity to discharge our duties. Yet his own political theory forbids any challenge to existing law. Recent neo-kantian philosophy has taken a different direction in this respect.

In neo-kantian political philosophy, beginning with John Rawls's *A Theory of Justice* (1971), the emphasis has been on the duty to uphold justice. This results in a much more permissive approach to civil disobedience. Rawls reasons that it is the justice of society that underpins the proscription of violence against government. So in authoritarian or tyrannical states these constraints on citizen conduct are lifted; while in 'nearly just' polities, citizens have rights to civil disobedience, with the requirement that they be willing to acknowledge the force and legitimacy of the constitution by submitting to due punishment. Subsequently, neo-kantian philosophers working on the idea of just war have put the duty to uphold justice together with the right to self-defence, and the right even to pre-emptive attack on an aggressor in order to prevent injustice, in a way that justifies certain instances of more energetic violent action than civil disobedience. A person who is non-culpably attacked by another has a right to defence. The assailant has forfeited her right not to be assaulted or harmed. There is no need to wait for the assailant to actually harm the victim, either. Providing that the judgement is reasonable that injury to the victim is imminent unless there is intervening action, injury to a potential assailant is justifiable, with the further constraint that the harm done to the assailant must be proportional to the threatened harm to the victim. This kind of argument has been used to justify the use of force for humanitarian purposes, even when its legal authority in national or international law is shaky, as in the case of the 1999 NATO bombings of Serbia in response to the ethnic cleansing of the Albanian population in Kosovo.

Clearly there is always room for a good deal of argument about the exact circumstances and limits, both in cases that are literally self-defence or defence of another from a dangerous aggressor, and in cases where revolutionary violence against the state, and in particular against state rulers, is being justified by analogy with the right to defence. James II's allies and defenders disputed that their man was a danger to the state. The familiar picture of armed military and police forces, in armoured vehicles, deploying water cannon or tear gas against demonstrators, some of whom are hurling stones towards the security positions, can clearly be analysed in the terms of the argument from self-defence, although there will be arguments about who began the violent action on any occasion. Proponents of diversity of tactics in the context of anti-globalization actions argue that the conduct and self-presentation of security forces, at actions and demonstrations, mean that a commitment to non-violence is only likely to eliminate direct political action and demonstration altogether, because techniques of crowd control by security authorities simply are violent, and effectively make demonstration in its traditional democratic sense impossible.

Conclusion

Could consequentialist reasoning justify the violent actions of Italian, Irish and other similar militant groups against liberal capitalist governments and societies in the 1970s or today? As we have seen, rather than consequences as such, philosophers like Honderich focus on intentions and goals of action, weighed against probabilities of success and against the failure of other less damaging means. Ex ante, probabilities of success can only be computed in the frame of theories of state, society, capital, class and so on, and it is certainly not plausible that the campaigns of murder and bombing could have worked out as the perpetrators imagined and planned. Ex post, from the point of view of history, it is also very unclear how we should weigh the outcomes of the counterfactual world in which the IRA did not organize itself and act as it did against the world that we have; or how to compute the costs of governmental, social and organized political, including violent, action against its products. In any case, consequentialist reasoning looks insufficiently robust as ex ante justification.

Can rights theory justify the execution of Charles I, or the force used against the French king in 1789? Lockean rights permit self-defence and defence of others, and also the punishment of aggressors in conditions when the political power underpinning state institutions has failed. Against patriarchal theory, and absolutist theory of authority, rights theorists assert the permissibility of action against sovereign authority when the sovereign forfeits his rights. These theorists assert the permissibility of harm to aggressors when aggressors imminently threaten harm to innocents, who must be defended or rescued. It is notable, however, that Locke, Kant and recent rights theorists all use the analogies of self-defence, rescue, and harm to culpable aggressors in individualistic terms. They insist that individual violent actors must be bound by rights and duties: they must independently assess the rightness of their actions in terms of defence, rescue and punishment. But political violence more commonly takes place when individuals act in institutional roles – as members of political groups, or as soldiers in armies (either literally, or as participants in a 'war' against injustice).

Within these justificatory arguments, violence is taken more or less for granted as the physical assault on and damage to another person, with the use of various weapons including the attacker's own body. The understanding of violence here is straightforwardly instrumental; the violence is independent of the meaning of the actions. Those actions are understood as defending the defenceless, rescuing the needy, punishing the transgressor, achieving an outcome of liberation or equality, or waging war. In the next chapter, we will see some of these themes continuing to work through rather different understandings of the meaning and scope of political violence, the relation between ends and means and the modes through which violence can be justified.

3

Complicating Matters

Introduction

This chapter complicates the previous chapter's story of political violence and ways in which it may be justified. It examines a range of examples and arguments from thinkers, predominantly from revolutionary traditions of thought influenced by marxism and existentialism, but beginning with political realists. All of these see violence as intrinsic to politics, but nevertheless seek to distinguish between acceptable and unacceptable forms of political violence. Criteria for making these distinctions challenge consequentialist arguments and rights-based accounts considered in the previous chapter. Instead they develop justificatory discourses that invoke criteria of necessity, virtue, style and creativity. In these perspectives, we find not only alternative justificatory accounts, but also alternative understandings of the relations between means and ends and of the nature of political violence.

Realism

Niccolò Machiavelli, in *The Prince* (1532), tells many stories of skilful and ruthless rulers who use charm, strategy, military prowess and violence in order to enhance their standing in the eyes of the people they rule, and to secure their historical reputation. One of the recurrent figures in Machiavelli's book is Cesare Borgia, the son of Pope Alexander VI, who was Machiavelli's contemporary and sought to conquer and establish control over a swathe of Italian territory. In one episode, Borgia was engaged in imposing his authority over an anarchic area of Italy, characterized by widespread brigandage, factionalism and abuse. In order to secure obedience to sovereign authority Borgia appointed one of his officers, a 'cruel efficient man' (Ramiro de Lorca), who pacified the region using plenipotentiary powers – of police enforcement, arrest, punishment and execution. At that point Borgia realized that he could benefit, in terms of strengthening his grip over the region and gaining popular support, by condemning de Lorca's excessive rule and 'liberating' the people from it, disavowing de Lorca's cruelty. So de Lorca's body was found cut in two pieces on the piazza. This story is of a familiar political move – bringing about or being implicated in a worse policy, in order that one's subsequent bad policy looks better by comparison. It is also a story of exemplary vivid violence – another familiar political move.

It's difficult to think of justification, in any valid logical sense of the term, in connection with such spectacular violence. For Machiavelli, violence is an element of the reality of government, of states. His emphasis is always on strategy, and he takes it for granted that violence is a means of maintaining territory and rule over the people in it. For Machiavelli, as in the twentieth century for Max Weber in *Economy and Society* (1921), states are built on violence – that is to say on the domination, by a group, of a territory, and the people and material resources within it; and violence continues to be the main means of political rule. Violence is not the only means: religious authority, economic monopoly and rent, exploitation of labour, popular support and consent, and many others are used in and by government. But under it all, states (or rulers) monopolize legitimate violence – as we saw in connection with Hobbes, sovereign authority includes getting to say who can use what violence against whom in what circumstances. At the same time, both Machiavelli and Weber emphasize that political action, violent or otherwise, is always risky and will inevitably generate unintended consequences.

Machiavelli and Weber deny that justification for political action, violent or non-violent, can be a matter of adherence to moral values such as goodness, or rights or duty, since such values are not necessarily related to the furtherance of political goods. In fact, both argue that the politically right thing to do may often clash with what is morally right. Nor can it be a matter of consequences alone, since the outcomes of action are always uncertain. Nevertheless, neither of them categorizes all instances of violence in politics as the same; rather they both find alternative ways of distinguishing between 'better' and 'worse' political violence. Borgia's cruelty is not simple cruelty, in Machiavelli's eyes, because it is not purely gratuitous, but reflects distinctively political virtues (those of a leader) as well as honourable political aims. The spectacular execution of de Lorca unites and consolidates a polity, in ways that will enable order, liberty and prosperity for the people under Borgia's rule as well as power and glory for himself. For Machiavelli greatness, as disclosed by the lives of the people but more importantly by historical significance, is the key aim of political life, and such greatness requires the capacity to found, maintain and nourish political community. Although such outcomes cannot be guaranteed, from Machiavelli's point of view, Borgia, in acting as he did, and for the reasons that he did, used violence well.

For Machiavelli and Weber the criteria for distinguishing between justified and unjustified action in politics, including violence, have to do with the kind of people we are, *how* we act both individually and collectively rather than *what* we do or even the outcomes of what we do. Weber is seized by the conflicts over values in his time, in particular the claims of rights and popular sovereignty, and the needs for justice. But for him, even though he is strongly committed to liberal values, it can't be the realization of those values that is the mark of legitimacy, but rather our individual and collective conduct in political struggle. In refusing to say that violence is justified if it is for justice or good, and wrong if it is for evil, justified if in accord with rights and duties, wrong if not, neither Machiavelli nor Weber gives up on the project of distinguishing good and bad violence altogether. The manner of its doing – whether it is done with courage and honour, whether it confirms the greatness of the polity that is its vehicle – becomes the criterion. Machiavelli condemns brutal cruelty, inhumanity, treachery, pitilessness, and he can value Borgia as ruler over de Lorca, rating Borgia's violence as recognisably virtuous where de Lorca's is just cruel. Weber condemns thoughtlessness, irresponsibility, free riding on others' courage. He endorses properly political power wielded by individuals who recognize its inseparability from violence, and condemns those who pusillanimously pretend that there is no violence in the state.

In the work of these realist thinkers we find three distinct discourses of justification for political violence. First, there is strategic justification. Justified political violence is violence which can plausibly be shown to be motivated by a desire to further distinctively political goods (which are not the same as moral values) such as order, liberty and prosperity. Second, there is virtue justification. Justified political violence is violence that displays characteristics of judgement, courage and resilience in the face of the possibility of one's own likely mistakes, failure and defeat. Third, there is aesthetic justification. Justified political violence is stylish or tragic, the spectacular sleight of hand of the political impresario, or the heroic assertion of the will of the individual in the face of overwhelming odds.

Necessity

In many ways, Karl Marx's dictum in the *Manifesto of the Communist Party* (1848) that 'all history is the history of class struggle', and that every epoch is marked by more or less violent conflict over control of the means of production, and hence control over the state, fits clearly in a realist tradition of thinking. In his case, however, he is as impatient with a focus on aesthetics, or character and virtue, as he is with a focus on values such as justice as criteria for distinguishing between permissible and impermissible political violence. For him, it can only be history that is the criterion of judgement: has political action, whether violent, coercive or otherwise, been material in the development of a classless society? For later generations of marxists, however, this question took on a rather different character. In this section and the next, we consider the arguments of thinkers influenced by marxism but also by French existentialist philosophy, a mode of thinking that rejects the idea that there are pre-existing criteria that determine the justifiability of political action.

Maurice Merleau-Ponty published *Humanism and Terror* in 1947 against the background of the (finally) successful French resistance to the nazi occupation of 1940–4, and the stalinist purges of the 1920s and 1930s in the Union of Soviet Socialist Republics (USSR). Between 1936 and 1938 numerous 'old Bolsheviks' (people who had been involved in the original revolutionary development of the communist party), and others who either were or were said to be sympathetic to the Trotskyist position on how the revolution should be pursued, were arrested, interrogated, in many cases tortured so that they 'informed' or 'confessed', publicly tried and then executed. Many more opponents or suspected opponents of the regime, of course, weren't subject to any trial at all, but died in custody or were extra-judicially executed.

Although at the time of the trials diplomatic commentators, journalists and others took it to be quite plausible that those on trial had in some legally valid sense 'endangered the state' (treason being an intrinsic condition of sovereignty), by 1938 there was widespread criticism of the sheer numbers of executions. Many erstwhile members of European communist parties resigned. Others endorsed the stalinist argument that defence of the revolution makes extreme measures necessary, and justified. Merleau-Ponty's essays were an attempt to make sense between the polarized positions of anti-communism (which effectively meant being in favour of United States-style capitalism and Cold War anti-communism), and pro-communism (which effectively meant blindness to the nature of Stalin and stalinism). The essays were also prompted by the publication in 1940 and reception of Arthur Koestler's *Darkness at Noon*, which fictionalized the context of terror and trials, focusing on the character Rubashov, who has many similarities to the real historical figure Nikolai Bukharin. Bukharin had been a close colleague of Lenin and Trotsky, was tried with others, and was shot in March 1938.

Merleau-Ponty's essays are based on the key idea that a regime which is liberal 'can be oppressive in reality, and that the case can be made that a regime which acknowledges its violence might have in it more genuine humanity'. He claims that capitalism, colonialism and imperialism all rely on violence; and the society that they aim to establish will, by definition, always rely on violence, although that violence can be (and is) mystified. The question he is concerned with is: what might be the place of violence in a revolutionary and developmental process that is aimed at the establishment of a cooperative, egalitarian society that does not rely on violence?

There is, of course, profound disagreement about ends: all political positions can frame their programmes in terms of ideals of justice or what is right. But this isn't the main problem with means–ends reasoning, according to Merleau-Ponty. For him, means–ends reasoning cannot do the job some philosophers think it can, because we can't really speak of 'ends'. At least, we can only do so in abstraction. This is because our ends and our intentions are transformed, once we turn them into actions. To talk of what our ends are, in advance of our engagement, can be idealistic. But because our engagement affects, changes, the nature of our abstract ends, it is impossible to weigh up ends against means. We can't endorse, says Merleau-Ponty, the kind of necessity reasoning that is articulated by figures like the stalinists who say, 'the revolution must be defended, the state must be secured against its enemies, by any means possible'. The futurity of 'ends', and the contingency of the outcomes of human actions and interactions, mean that the ends of our actions, or the outcomes of the intentions we form now, can't be weighed against the consequences of our actions, except with historical hindsight. So this doesn't help those who are making decisions and judgements now.

He turns to the case of Bukharin to help cast light

on the implication of thinking about the relation between means and ends in a non-instrumental way. Bukharin, according to Merleau-Ponty's reading of the trial testimony, first, maintained his personhood in his speech asserting himself as a responsible individual. Second, he rejected the imputation of espionage and sabotage. Third, he engaged with the ambiguity of what he had done. He did not say that relative to the frame of the USSR it amounted to endangering the revolution, whereas relative to the frame of the 1917 revolution it amounted to honourable conduct. That is, he did not try to weigh up two alternative bases for ethics. Instead, Bukharin recognized the 'ambiguity that risks condemnation' in his conduct. In stalinist USSR there could be no toleration of ambiguity, which, itself, was criminal treason. But, for Merleau-Ponty, Bukharin's affirmation of ambiguity in some sense exemplifies the freedom that the violence of the revolution is purported to serve. Contrary to stalinist clarity – so deadly in its condemnation of any dissent – we must fully acknowledge ambiguity.

Ambiguity is key also in Simone de Beauvoir's consideration, in *The Ethics of Ambiguity* (1948), of the paradoxes of political action, in the light of the context of French resistance to occupation and struggles for freedom. Neither Beauvoir nor

Merleau-Ponty says that violence is ubiquitous – not all forms of society, economy and polity are like fascism or capitalism. However, we can't think about the French resistance to nazism, or the Moscow trials, other than in the violent contexts apart from which they are inconceivable. This means, first, that the justification of violence cannot simply be a matter of weighing the balance. Second, our ethical indignation on behalf of Bukharin, or a resistance fighter, can't really be on the basis of the violence that is visited on them. Violence pervades the whole context. Third, then, violence is necessary.

This is not the same necessity, though, as means–ends reasoners and consequentialists invoke when they speak of 'by all means necessary' or 'in the last resort'. Rather, we must attend to how violent actors discharge their violence. Is this with the capacity to transcend necessity and express freedom? Or as creatures who are trapped and enmeshed in a situation not of their own making? For Merleau-Ponty and Beauvoir, we must refuse to be polarized in the ways that the uses of violence, whether by fascists, stalinists or capitalists, insist we be. In our necessary engagement with violence it is critical that we continue to refuse any simplistic 'are you with us or against us?' choices – 'choices' that are of course violently enforced. What we cannot do is disavow, or seek to conceal, the violence that we are enmeshed in and in the context of which we exert our agency and potentially make something new. In addition to echoing themes of necessity, virtue and aesthetics that we have already identified in realist traditions of political thought, Merleau-Ponty and Beauvoir introduce another strand of justificatory discourse in relation to violence. This is what we might call an expressive or creative strand, in which violence is justified to the extent that it expresses and instantiates as well as potentially furthers a particular value, in their case the value of freedom.

Liberation

A theme of necessity, and how actors conduct themselves with regard to it, is also central to the thinking about violence by Frantz Fanon, who was primarily concerned with the anti-colonial struggle, but was also, like Merleau-Ponty and Beauvoir, influenced by marxist and existentialist ideas. In 1958 Fanon represented the provisional government in exile of the Republic of Algeria. Since 1954, the Algerian war had been fought between the National Liberation Front (Front de Libération Nationale, FLN) and the French colonial military, police and administrative forces. In 1956 the FLN launched a campaign of guerrilla warfare against the French Algerian authorities, which escalated with reprisal actions by the authorities – the Battle of Algiers. The French government deployed troops to suppress the FLN in an exceptionally (for the time) brutal regime including torture and disappearances. As ambassador to independent Ghana, Fanon attended the All African People's Congress in Accra in December 1958. There he made a celebrated speech challenging the doctrine of non-violence that was influential among African leaders, including Kwame Nkrumah, president of Ghana. Fanon, who received a standing ovation and 'wild applause' (although he was not a leader of the Algerian delegation), told the conference that the struggle for liberation could never rule out recourse to violence; that freedom fighters and nationalist leaders had to adopt all forms of struggle, and could not rely on peaceful negotiations alone. Thereafter the idea that it is the context of violence itself, the violence of the colonial regimes and institutions, that determines uses of force and incidents of violence was influential among African leaders.

In *The Wretched of the Earth* (published in French in 1961) Fanon, at greater length, emphasizes the given, irreducibly violent context of colonial rule, and of the imposition of capitalist production and relations on economies and societies. Governing races arrive from elsewhere; they compartmentalize 'settler' and 'native' zones, the boundaries of which are violently policed; indigenous culture and society are crushed; native people are murdered. Given this, decolonization can only be a violent phenomenon. Living in such a context oppresses people, and it brutalizes them. Everyone is afraid. Colonized people fear and also are fascinated by the settlers, their brutality and their segregated lives. The colonialists cannot establish the levels of force necessary to thoroughly subdue all territory and people. So the threat of retaliatory violence is omnipresent to them. In such an atmosphere of violence – in particular at the point when native people begin to organize themselves in parties, when corporations want guarantees of order – aggression will be acted out, 'guns will go off by themselves'.

In his speech in Accra, Fanon called for political leaders not to rule out violence as a strategy and tactic in anti-colonialist and independence struggles. His argument was exhortatory and prescriptive. In *The Wretched of the Earth* he sets out a more predictive and explanatory theory of violence, according to which there will be stages of action and reaction, colonial violence and liberatory violence.

The overwhelming brutality of colonial settlers and their defenders can't secure their rule; segregated spaces contribute to escalations of violence; politically organized elites and urban populations face the contradiction between the possibility of negotiation with the colonial powers and the reality of colonial violence. And so on. According to Fanon's presentation of his theory, violence is structured into the very fabric of the polity and economy. The 'structure' is not static, however. Human beings are actors and reactors – arrests of leaders will lead to protest; brutality can embolden as much as it cows its sufferers; people's hopes for justice push them to new understandings of injustice. This dynamic process means that the structure of violence shifts. In destroying traditional ways, the settlers don't petrify the natives, but, unwittingly, make space for new identities, new lives, to spring up.

The political ethics of violence, then, poses the question of how we engage in and with the violence that is necessary. Fanon bitterly criticizes political leaders who take on the ways of the colonial authorities they are seeking to overcome – using violence strategically against political opponents, self-interestedly using it tactically in defence of their own wealth and position. Like the colonists, these leaders seek to conceal this violence under a veneer of 'civilization', employing bureaucracy, bargaining with capitalist corporations, and organizing political discussion with points of order while employing violent agents at arm's length.

Fanon's argument, instead, is that revolutionary actors have to take and shape the violence that has been inflicted on them both to transform themselves and to create a new political community. Engagement in violence can enable the construction of new forms of subjectivity and agency – new senses of power, of assertion of self against oppression. The colonized must refuse to take on the bodily and social identities that are valued, seemingly, by those who dominate, exploit and enslave. In organizing themselves collectively in violent anti-colonial struggle, they can express and instantiate the values of collective commitment and mutual respect that will characterize the post-colonial condition.

Conclusion

What forms of violence can ideas of necessity justify? Philosophers of reality and necessity focus on the inescapability of violence in the forms and maintenance of states, and infer that we are licensed to judge some violent actions as virtuous while others are vicious, some as stylish and others as ugly, some as tragic and some as gratuitous. Marxist and existentialist thinkers emphasize that such value judgements trade productively on ambiguity. Resistance fighters who in the course of their violent assertions of self figure a new world of freedom give one meaning to violence; colonial administrators who use dogs and security personnel with batons to safeguard colonial living spaces, or mines whose value goes back to Europe, figure a degenerate world of oppression and exploitation. We must face the ambiguities of meaning of violence, and the necessity of violent acts, and wrest them from the powerful. For Beauvoir, our lives individually and collectively must be lived so that all such inflictions of violence can only possibly be understood as exercises of freedom for freedom. For Fanon, the oppressed must embrace the creative possibilities of violence in a world that is constructed to violently repress the self-worth of the colonized.

Thinkers such as Merleau-Ponty, Beauvoir and Fanon extend the repertoire of justifications of violence not only as a response to their rejection of consequentialist and rights-based arguments, but fundamentally because they have a distinct understanding of the nature of political violence. Although they continue to use elements of means–

ends thinking in their arguments, they are much more concerned about how means transform ends, and about the significance of unintended consequences, than the thinkers considered in chapter 2. As well as introducing us to new ways of justifying political violence, therefore, they also force us to think again about the subject matter of this book. In the next chapter, we will return to the question of the meaning of political violence, and in chapter 5 to how consideration of that meaning puts the justificatory strategies explored in this and the previous chapter into question.

4

The Meaning of Political Violence

Introduction

The arguments considered in chapter 3 challenged assumptions about political violence that we found at work in chapter 2. These arguments are critical not only of moral justifications of political violence, but of the very idea that such violence can be understood in instrumental terms, as a tool for politics, that might be chosen or not. In emphasizing the necessity of violence, they also call attention to the ways violence might be systematically entrenched in structures of domination, and challenge the idea that political violence can be described solely in terms of particular actions or series of actions on the part of individual agents. At the same time, they introduce a set of alternative justificatory discourses beyond moral or strategic considerations, in which 'good' violence can be distinguished from 'bad' by reference to arguments from virtue, aesthetics, style or creativity. In this chapter we return to questions raised in chapter 1 about the meaning of political violence, and how different understandings of that meaning might affect the persuasiveness of any of the justificatory moves that we have so far considered.

Structure

So far, we have approached the question of the justification of political violence by considering episodes: fights between anti-capitalism protestors and security personnel; the French revolution; the Moscow arrests, trials and executions; IRA terrorism; anti-colonial violence; the Italian, French and German resistances to nazism and fascism; and so on. These episodes consist, in this kind of historical analysis, of numerous acts of interpersonal violence, and numerous sufferings, injuries and deaths by the recipients of that violence. This is what Slavoj Žižek has referred to, in *Violence: Six Sideways Reflections* (2008), as 'subjective' violence – violence that is enacted and experienced, by people, as such. When we think of violence in this way we think of an agent who violently inflicts a blow, a recipient who cannot escape it, and the magnitude, so to speak, of the violence is measured by the force used and, critically, by the injury done. We think, for example, of the arrest, ill-treatment and shooting of Bukharin; or of the Battle of Algiers.

However, this 'subjective' concept of violence has been argued to offer only part of the story. Johan Galtung famously argued in *Essays in Peace Research* (1975) that the *real* problem of violence is not direct, subjective violence, but the *structural* violence that both underpins and exceeds it. For Galtung, the exemplary cases of structural violence are poverty and imperialism. These are the economic and political structures that underpin subjective violence, in the sense of structurally positioning the resources to use violence, but also providing reasons why subordinated agents turn to violence. More than this, however, the toll of death, injury and dispossession inflicted by structures of poverty and imperialism is greater than what follows even from the most destructive acts of direct violence. Here we can see echoes of the arguments of thinkers discussed in the previous chapter, in particular Fanon's identification of colonialism as inherently violent, whether direct violence is taking place or not. Žižek adopts the alternative term 'objective' violence to capture the same point that Galtung is making.

In Žižek's analysis, you can't see the subjective violence except by defocusing from the objective violence that is the background. And vice versa: if we bring the objective violence into focus, we defocus from the subjective violence of interpersonal conflict. Historians, analogously, critically analyse the way we individuate a series of actions and interactions into an 'event' like the Italian 'years of lead' of the 1970s, the English civil wars, or the Battle of Algiers. Of course, in some such cases, there is a declaration – such as was made on the liberation of Paris, when French people and Allied troops celebrated in the streets on 25 August 1944. The date then lives on, in memory, in photographs, in anniversaries and so on. But whether it is declared, or whether the date is the eventual outcome of lots of historical study, this is only by breaking into the continuous flow of processes and interactions, fixing a moment as 'the beginning', another as the end. This is a matter of epistemic interruption and convention, sedimented in history textbooks and reference websites. In stating the dates of the Battle of Algiers as August 1956 to September 1957 we focus on what, with hindsight, is a plausible first event – although that could well be the execution of

FLN prisoners in June 1956, or the reprisals against the European population by the FLN in the days that followed. We have to ignore, or not know about, all the ways that the days and months before and after were continuous with, similar to, just as conflictual for some people, just as ordinary for others.

The question of structural, or objective, violence pervades the thinking and writing of many thinkers and activists. For Fanon, as we have seen, colonialism – moving into other people's countries, extracting goods and resources by mining and taking agricultural produce away, not paying the people who live in the land to begin with and whose labour is exploited to get the goods anything like the value of their work, enforcing new economic, cultural and political relations – is violent in its very inception, not just when cities are brutally policed, laws violently enforced, challengers and non-cooperators viciously punished. In fact, the violence of colonialism is most effectively deployed, familiarly, when those who are subjugated concur with the rightness of the subjugation – seeking perhaps to emulate the ways of the colonizers, internalizing the exploiters' view of who is superior and who inferior. Theorists such as Pierre Bourdieu, in *The Logic of Practice* (1980), have called these processes – whose outcomes in terms of injury and disadvantage are as grave as the outcomes of physical attack – symbolic violence. A woman who believes that as a woman she is rightly subservient to men's judgements and claims is disadvantaged and injured without being hit.

From the point of view of critics of structural and symbolic violence, as political agents we have to bring the invisible, systemic violence into focus, and our political efforts have to be directed at busting the structures, and challenging the meanings, that currently enmesh and constrain us. Politics has to secure new distributions – of rights and duties, of goods like honour and social prestige, as well as of nutrition, education, work, income, wealth and capital. For thinkers like Galtung, this must be a matter of governmental and inter-governmental action, in tandem with transformations in the cultural systems of norms and symbols that deem some distributions right and proper (e.g. it is wrong for girls to go to school) in the direction of egalitarian justice (e.g. so that girls are not wronged in this way: girls are educated as boys are, so that they are able to defend their and others' rights, and work as full citizens and denizens of the world for a flourishing life for all).

Politics

Thinkers such as Galtung rethink the idea of political violence in ways that expand what counts as violence. In contrast to this, Hannah Arendt limits the meaning of the concept of violence to direct 'subjective' violence, but challenges the ways in which 'political' is normally understood. Arendt was a German-Jewish refugee whose work was primarily concerned with understanding the genocidal elimination of human difference and diversity by the totalitarian regimes of fascism, nazism and stalinism. Her text *On Violence*, published in 1969, responds to contemporary events. It is a contribution to the controversy about the student protests that erupted in European and US universities in 1968 and were still continuing. In New York, where Arendt lived and worked, students at Columbia University protested, from 1967, over university links with the research–military–industrial network of institutions implicated one way or another in the war in Vietnam. There were also protests about the university's implication in racial segregation in its neighbourhood. Protestors occupied university buildings in March 1968; the occupation was violently ended by New York police on 30 April, in an operation which lasted more than twenty-four hours, and saw about 150 people injured and 700 protestors arrested.

In Arendt's response to these events, and more broadly to traditions of thinking about violence in politics, she criticizes predominant ways of thinking about political violence. As we have seen, a common understanding of violence as political is that it is directed to political ends. The students wanted Columbia University explicitly to disengage from any kind of segregationist urban or architectural development. They wanted the university explicitly to disengage from any activity connected to the US government's war and military policy and machine. They wanted the US government to end the Vietnam War, and turn onto a path of non-warfare-based humane policy. Any violence that occurs in the process of campaigning, demonstrating, prosecuting these arguments for public policy is, on this account, 'political' violence, because it is for political ends. A second common way of understanding political violence is when violence is thought of as a specific political means. We can petition, lobby, campaign to raise public awareness or to change public opinion; we can run for office or support particular candidates or parties; we can demonstrate, march, occupy, sit down, stand up. And we can use violence: so far in this book we have met instances of sabotage of key economic sites like factories; destruction of key public sites like shopping centres or pubs; kidnap of notable individuals; fighting back against police and security personnel who try to enforce laws, or to direct demonstrators; and assassinations. This too is 'political violence' – violence as a political means.

But Arendt dissents: for her, the phrase 'political violence' is a contradiction in terms. To begin with, the very idea of ends and means is hardly applicable in politics, which by definition is a realm of human action and relations which is non-instrumentalist, and the outcomes of which are unpredictable. Political power – the capacities that people have when they act in concert – cannot be directed to particular ends. The point of it is the process, the relations, the being together engaging in public affairs – visibly, audibly, thinking about the implications for all. According to this meaning of political power and political action, legislation and administration aren't themselves political. They, rather, secure the 'space' within which we can act together to maintain the polity. Thinking in first-person self-interested terms isn't political either. We do this when, as economic actors, we decide how much we are willing to spend on a certain good, or which of alternative investments is the better one. As soon as we start thinking about everyone in our economic lives – campaigning against blood diamonds, for instance, or for fair trade in cash commodities – we have ceased to be 'pure' economic actors and we have become political. In politics there are no 'final' decisions. Today's decision, for example in the form of legislation about fair trade, is the impetus for political action that reopens the question. This openness and space for creativity are what, for Arendt, is specific about politics.

In contrast, in her view, violence destroys. It can – in assassination, or execution, or massacre – have a horribly 'final' quality. It is always instrumentalist: we are violent to defend ourselves, or to express our fear or frustration or other emotion, or to injure or kill. This bodily, affective quality of violence is a critical aspect of it. Any 'instrumentalism' is only, and always, immediate and short-term. The tyrant is dead, the emotions are spent. Sometimes, Arendt argues, violence is the only way. In a sense, she concedes a kind of 'necessity' argument. She concedes that ethics, the need to be able to live with oneself, might mean that, in a situation of great injustice, killing the tyrant (or its equivalent) is the only way. But this is the stuff of tragedy. The tyrant is dead, the emotions are spent – but the ramifications will ripple on. Trauma can be – will be – communicated through social contexts and networks and across generations. After the initial effects, all is unpredictable: escalation, retaliation, reaction, revenge, vendetta. Violence can – does tend to – overwhelm anyone who uses it intentionally, and to overwhelm any putatively political ends it purports to serve. The only likely outcome of the use of violence, however good the purpose, on Arendt's account, is more violence.

Of course, history tells us that sometimes wars can exhaust all the combatants, and kill relevant ones. Undoubtedly, an event like the death of Hitler by assassination might have opened an opportunity for new political relations and thinking within the German command; just as the actual death of Hitler by suicide undoubtedly meant that something changed for those who were left. But whereas there can be political reason – genuinely political reason – to engage in dialogue, or to float an idea for a new way of organizing or instituting some human need or function, to make a speech, to try to work together in a new way, there cannot possibly be political reason to engage in violence. The outcomes of violence, according to Arendt, are so dangerous, costly and injurious that it cannot be just one possible technique in our political repertoire.

Arendt's critical view of the violent student protestors in 1968–9, then, was that far from acting politically they were engaging in conduct which was antithetical to politics. The nazis, the stalinists and the fascists, similarly, have to be judged not only on the vast human suffering and destruction they unleashed – to be sure, that was apocalyptic in its scale, and we might think that there is no more to be said. But for Arendt it matters that the apocalyptic violence was intended to destroy human diversity and individuality; and it matters that it was intended to destroy the spaces for politics. Stalin's refusal to hear any view, any voice, other than his own is anti-political, as well as being despicable because he unleashed such extreme violence on individuals, groups and whole populations. Arendt's fears about the nuclear arsenal, similarly, were that not only do we now all live in the shadow of the possible annihilation of life on earth, but that the magnitude of this threat was threatening the polity. When government leaders can speak of reason of state, insisting on secrecy and high levels of security, openness itself is threatened. This threat to political space, to the possibility of genuine participation in making the world that we inhabit – because of secrecy, because the potential forces of violence are so overwhelming – is a serious threat. All violence – whether it is prosecuted by the state against citizens and denizens, or by political activists against the state – threatens to destroy politics.

Arendt's argument, then, goes deep in respect of 'political violence'. There can never be a political justification for political violence. Violence can be aimed at political goals – the FLN challenged the French colonial power and asserted the Algerian aspiration for independence, seeking to show the French colonists that they could not rule and extract goods from the country, except at a prohibitively high price; Stalin succeeded, for a time, in suppressing all potential internal opposition to the regime. Or violence can have political effects, as it happens. The generation of 1968 ran up against contradictions between the aspiration to freedom and peace, and the embodiment and institutionalization, in culture and in political institutions like the movements and parties, of sexism, and specifically sexual violence. This generated a new 'wave' of feminist action. This was not intended by the main participants in the students' movement, or in the connected movement for Black power. But new forms of feminism are among the most significant of the emergent outcomes of 1968. These connections between violence and politics are undeniable.

But Arendt's argument is that violence is destructive of political life. If a polity is suffused with security and secrecy, as Stalin's USSR was, then open political life and world building are impossible. Institutions and public life can be destroyed by distrust, by policing, by the polarization that violent action engenders. If opposition to unjust or brutal rule is prosecuted only by violence, then the capacities for political action are stymied and thwarted. When the violence ends, a political peace will be fearsomely difficult to build.

Practice

Galtung's concept of structural violence and Arendt's argument for drawing a clear line between politics and violence illuminate different aspects of the constituent terms of the expression 'political violence'. Galtung displaces attention onto objective or structural as opposed to subjective or agentic violence; Arendt treats violence as a (highly dangerous and unreliable) tool, as opposed to the creative and indeterminate character of politics. This is in contrast to an alternative way of analysing the meaning of political violence, to be found in the work of Fanon, and in feminist thought, particularly the work of Elaine Scarry, which focuses on unpacking political violence as a practice that itself produces subjectivities, and that depends on and instantiates political relations, regardless of the purposes for which the violence is being used.

As we saw in chapter 3, Fanon argues for the necessity and potentially liberating quality of anti-colonial violence. Nevertheless, in the final chapter of *The Wretched of the Earth*, drawing on his experience as a practising psychiatrist in Algeria, he describes the experience and effects of violence in ways that undermine any straightforward celebration of it. He charts the presuppositions and effects of violence, psychological, emotional, social and physical, for perpetrators and victims. He shows how the practice of violence as a political technique is secured only by the production of particular kinds and relations of subjects; that is to say, subjects who are only able to live with themselves through various kinds of dissociation from their past experience and actions, manifested in a variety of neuroses and psychoses, and who struggle to live with either 'friend' or 'enemy' others. Here, the political and existential promise of violence, in relation to strategic gains, to virtue and to creativity, is confronted by the experience of violence as not only profoundly disabling, but instantiating a politics of hierarchy and exclusion. From the torturers' transposition of his relation to his victims in the cells to his relation with his wife and daughters at home, to a child's assumption that his friend, because he is one of the colonizers, must be killed, the political relations inherent in violence range from those of abjection and exploitation, to those of mutually exclusive friend-or-enemy identities.

Elaine Scarry in *The Body in Pain: The Making and Unmaking of the World* (1985) particularly focuses on the embodied experience of violence for victims and perpetrators. Her accounts of practices of political violence such as interrogational torture put the body in pain at the centre. She emphasizes (from the evidence and testimony of victims of torture) how power works in the relationship between tortured and torturer. Contradictorily, the self is annihilated by pain, and yet the confession, or the information, is treated as that of a full agent. The only path to reachievement of selfhood for a torture victim is to abject herself, ingratiate herself, with the powerful agent. Phenomenologically, this aggrandized power is more real than the pain and suffering. As Scarry points out, to have great pain is to have absolute (first-person) certainty about it; but to hear about or see another's pain is to have (second- and third-person) doubt. So the first-person knowledge is not shareable. By contrast, there is no doubt about the domination of the regime over the tortured person. The suffering self, the annihilated self, the simultaneously responsible self and the torturer become the composite, certain, symbol of the regime's power.

Fanon, too, emphasizes the hierarchical political relation of state, over torturer, and over tortured. Torture is a transformative practice, for those who inflict it as well as for those who suffer it. The torturer who cannot escape the memories and flashbacks of the screams of his victims is positioned, by that practice, as a frustrated dominator in his household, as a hopeless friend and social being in his networks. In these accounts, torture instantiates an absolutely hierarchical political relation. It does not simply injure or annihilate some subjects, and reward others (with office, pay etc.). It produces those subjects.

Feminism famously made the personal political. Issues that had been assumed to be specific to private relations or to apolitical questions of subjective identity are actually intrinsic to, and produced by, political struggles for governance and control of human and non-human resources between masculinized (usually but not always men) and feminized (usually but not always women) actors. In recognizing that a key site of this power struggle was the production of subjective identity, feminist analysis from the start was interested in how violence produces subjective self-understanding, and both instantiates and embodies relations of power at the level of experience. Feminists have examined how gendered violences are experienced by women and men in different contexts. It has mapped and described the pain and trauma, the effects on self-worth and agency, and the shifting meanings of violence as victims survive (or not) and process (or not) their experiences. It has also focused explicitly on the experiences of empowerment, at least in the moment, on the part of perpetrators. In particular in cases of gang rape and rape in war, but also in cases of collective racist violence, feminists have shown how these practices rely on and build solidarity between men. They reinforce the identification of perpetrators with masculinity and of victims with femininity – whether the victims are men or women (and whether or not women are implicated in the perpetration). In this respect, although it is easy to see sex and gender violence in functional terms, the purpose of the violence is less important than its re-enactment and its institutionalization of a hierarchical, racialized and gendered, order.

As we have seen, it is quite common for forms of political violence to be conceptualized on analogy with war, including revolutionary and anti-state violence. For Fanon, for the IRA, for the Red Brigades, for the student activists of whom Arendt was critical, the turn to militancy in tactical terms articulated their perception of war – between colonizer and colonized, white and black, bourgeois and proletarian. In feminist analysis of war, a great deal of attention has been paid to how the practice and the justification of war are fundamentally gendered. To practise war requires that fighters are able to identify with their side in a conflict, and to kill, harm and risk injury and death on its behalf. Gender is a key technology for the production of such fighters. The abjection of effeminacy that forms part both of formal training and of the hazing practices within military units is closely connected to gender discrimination regarding who is qualified to fight. The masculinized qualities fighters are supposed to identify with in turn rest on childhood and adolescent socialization of males and females. Even where women or homosexual men are fighters, both in conventional and in revolutionary contexts, research has shown that such gender hierarchies do not disappear.

As do other forms of political violence, the practice of war exceeds its allegedly limited domain. It pervades societies which provide troops or are parties to conflict. Techniques of violence acquired in combat pervade social settings. Traumas are brought back home after conflicts, often in the form of sex and gender violence, in particular in domestic and kinship relations. In the field of combat itself, the carrying through of masculinized values and solidarity into practices of sexual and racialized violence, within military forces as well as against enemy others, is well documented.

The gendered politics of justifications of war is as striking as the centrality of gender to the practice of war. As feminist analysis has shown, the binary gender distinction is crucial to the production of political friend and foe, to the often racialized and religiously inflected identities in nationalist discourses, and to the production of ally and enemy in war. More generally, it articulates a manichaean, zero-sum understanding of 'us' versus 'them' within any conflict situation. In the so-called war on terror, the acceptability of exceptional measures, such as the interrogational torture of terrorist suspects, was legitimated in gendered terms. These suspects could be presented alternatively as hyper-masculinized, committed to unlimited violence and posing an imminent threat to innocent civilians; or as effeminate and cowardly beings, effectively subhuman and therefore unworthy of respect. The violence of the state was framed as paternal, protective and chivalrous. Similarly, the justification of the invasion of Afghanistan in 2001 was reinforced by a focus on the Taliban's treatment of women. This put the delinquent masculinity of the Taliban in contrast to the chivalrous, heroic masculinity of the US and its allies.

When political violence is conceived as practice, attention is focused on how individual actors are able to be violent, on the kinds of subjectivities produced by violence, and on the political relations inherent in violent engagement between embodied subjects. This phenomenological approach connects structural and symbolic violence with direct, subjective violence. It shows how systematic hierarchies enable but are also reproduced in the experience of violence, often as an unintended consequence. And it challenges the reduction of violence to a tool serving other purposes, whilst at the same time reinforcing Arendt's claim that violence is more closely associated with a project of domination than with politics as the open-ended creation of a world in common.

Conclusion

When it comes to structural violence, the grounds of justification are pushed back beyond specific violent events to the invisible structural relations that shape contemporary political possibilities for different groups of people. This move puts standard distinctions between violence and non-violence into question, challenges the idea that we can treat violence in politics as discrete episodes, and reinforces arguments from chapter 3 that violence is an ineradicable aspect of the world, even in the absence of direct killing and injuring. Such arguments can be used to justify the use of subjective revolutionary violence, and to challenge the legitimacy of any subjective violence deployed by the powerful, in the form of the state or the ruling class.

Arendt's clear distinction between violence and politics leads her to deny the possibility of political justifications for the use of violence. Although she concedes that violence may occasionally bring about justice, she argues that this is only likely to be possible when there is a definite, short-term wrong to be righted. Violence is instrumental in character and has to be judged in those terms. Politics, however, is a distinctively public and collective mode of action in freedom, which is in principle open-ended and unpredictable. To bring violence into the political realm is to destroy that realm.

Arendt's treatment of violence in instrumental terms, like that of many of the thinkers discussed in chapters 2 and 3, brackets out consideration of violence as itself a practice. When thinkers such as Fanon or Scarry analyse the experience and repercussions of participation in violence for actual human beings, whether as perpetrators or victims, they suggest not only that violence has damaging transformative effects on those caught up in it, but also that it relies on and reproduces relations of hierarchy between different actors. From the point of view of feminist thinkers, any justification of political violence needs to take account of what violence is and does directly to victims, and to perpetrators, regardless of the purposes it is meant to serve, or the courage or style with which it is carried out.

5

Against the Justification of Political Violence

Introduction

In chapter 2 we saw that consequentialist, rights-based and duty-based arguments rely on being able to, as it were, separate the violence from the politics. Violence is understood in neutrally instrumental terms, and as distinct from the ends, rights or values that it serves. These arguments treat violence as, in principle, a reliable option for action. Description of the action is unaffected by the violence that is enacted. The action is defined, and its success or failure is judged, in terms of its outcomes, intentions or goals. We also noted how descriptions of politically violent actions often rely on analogies which then pervade the justificatory discourse. If certain types of politically violent action are deemed analogous to actions within war, to rescue, or to individual self-defence or other defence, then this becomes part of the account of in what circumstances these types of action could be justified. Violence is deemed neither to pervade the political action, nor to be included in its description. Yet the tropes of war, defence and civil rescue pervade descriptions of the political situations in which violence is justified.

In chapter 3, we considered justificatory arguments that start from the very distinct premises that political violence is necessary rather than optional. The thinkers who present violence this way tend to emphasize, however, that it cannot be trusted reliably to deliver what is intended, and that it pervades both the context of political action and the nature of the action itself. In contrast to the arguments considered in chapter 2, justifications of political violence from these perspectives are much more about discriminating between more and less, good and bad, violence. And, as we saw, such discriminations are arrived at in relation to diverse criteria beyond the strategic: for example, criteria of virtue, linked to questions of worthiness of character; aesthetic criteria, linked to questions of style or genre; or expressive or creative criteria, in which the transformative, liberatory character of the decision to use violence is the mark of its justifiability.

The arguments discussed in chapter 4 further

problematize instrumental justifications of political violence. First, the idea of 'structural violence' puts the individuation of violence into discrete episodes into question, and blurs clear distinctions between violence and non-violence. Second, Arendt's argument that violence is fundamentally anti-political rules out the possibility of *political* justifications for the use of violence, and considerably narrows the possibility of retrospective moral justification. Third, the phenomenology of violent practice brings into the analysis a range of factors that most justifications of the use of violence in politics tend to bracket out. In this chapter, we return to the question of justification directly, and examine arguments in justification of state violence in the context of anti-state terrorism, anti-colonial violence and anti-capitalist violence. We demonstrate how, in each case, arguments elaborated in chapter 4 affect the force of arguments first encountered in chapters 2 and 3. We conclude that political violence can never be justified.

State

After the deadly attacks on New York City and Washington DC on 11 September 2001, the United

States administration engaged in arguments about the use of torture in the interrogation of terrorist suspects. These were rehearsed in the notorious 'torture memos' produced in the office of the US Attorney General in 2002. State violence, as we have seen, has historically been justified in terms of the necessary maintenance of social order, and the imperative of the defence of the realm, its territory and its people. The memos addressed two questions. What kinds of infliction of suffering might be permissible in order to gain knowledge about actual or potential terrorist attacks? Should the state regulate the practice of torture, by issuing torture warrants to the security services when judges deemed it right? The context of the torture memos, and of the subsequent controversy, was the zero-sum definition of the 'war on terror'. The binary language of war (them or us, friend or enemy, good or evil) was important both for the definition of the threat being faced by the US, and for the (attempted) justification of exceptional measures to deal with the threat.

The publication of the torture memos reinvigorated broader ethical and political debates about the state's pre-emptive, or preventive, use of violence in pursuit of goals of collective self-defence and the rule of law. In these controversies the 'ticking terrorist bomb' scenario has become a staple of jurisprudential and hypothetical ethical reasoning. Suppose there is a captured terrorist who is known to know the location of a bomb which is timed to go off within a short space of time, killing a large number of innocent people. Some politicians and philosophical thinkers argue that, in this situation, the use of torture on the terrorist is justifiable if it is the only way that he or she can be got to divulge the location of the bomb. The argument has recourse to last resort: suppose that normal interview and interrogation techniques have failed. In straightforwardly consequentialist terms, saving many innocent lives outweighs the harm to the guilty terrorist. If it were a question of killing one in order to save hundreds, the answer, in this frame of reasoning, seems clear – killing one is justified. But a dead terrorist cannot disclose, whereas a tortured one can. Contributions to the debate also rest on theories of right and duty: the terrorist, by threatening innocent others, has forfeited her right to immunity from physical assault.

Some objections to the argument for torture accept one or other of these reasoning principles, but reach different conclusions. Consequentially, it is disputed whether torture is an efficient, or even effective at all, method of extracting reliable information. From a rights point of view, a terrorist has certainly forfeited some rights, but it is argued that the right not to be tortured is distinct from the right not to be harmed or imprisoned. It has been argued that inflicting great suffering on someone who has not been subject to legal trial and found guilty undermines the rule of law. Such arguments, if successful, conclude that torture is not justified in this scenario.

Other objections put the justificatory frameworks themselves into question. The 'ticking terrorist bomb' scenario incorporates a number of simplified assumptions. It presumes an individual perpetrator. It presumes that the potential torturers have perfect, or very highly probably correct, information. It presumes that the outcomes of the torture, and of subsequent actions to defuse the bomb, to divert potential victims from danger and so on, are all within the control of the relevant officers and agents – that is, torture is thought of as an instrument designed to fulfil certain functions and discharge certain tasks. It assumes that torture is not the worst thing – it is no worse than killing, for example. All of these have been subjected to extended criticism.

First, in actual cases of urban warfare and terrorism it is not individual perpetrators, but networks of associates, kin and cultural community members who are the subjects presumed to have relevant knowledge. The targeting, interrogating and sometimes, as we know, torturing of networks is a qualitatively and quantitatively different phenomenon from the idealized, limited, permissible torture of the scenario. Political actions, violent or non-violent, are not fundamentally individual matters. Given this, although the potential victims of the bomb are presented, in the scenario, as innocents, actually, political allegiance and identification being what they are, they are likely to include some who are party to, or sympathetic to, the cause of the terrorist. Second, the scenario makes the familiar simplifying assumption of confidence or certainty in the state officers' knowledge of the captured terrorist's knowledge. But this epistemic assumption does not plausibly model knowledge in political contexts, where it is expected there will be errors, confusions, misidentifications, shifting allegiances and identities, and the deliberate production of misinformation on all sides.

Third, the scenario depends on a model of political action in which the infliction of pain will reveal the secret of the bomb's location, and the authorities will then be able to defuse it and save the lives of threatened innocents. Beyond obvious scepticism – that tortured persons may get the information wrong, or they may say what they think their torturers want them to say, or time may run out anyway – critics take issue with this single-path analysis, with its intended and foreseeable consequences. Revelation of the United States' internal debates about the permissibility and uses of torture became part of the justifications for insurgencies in Afghanistan and Iraq. Rather than serving to neutralize well-identified threats to the state, this path of reason and action had consequences that were quite out of the control of those presiding over the torture policies, serving to confirm terrorists' views of the nature of the US regime, and to put members of target communities firmly into the subject position of dissociation from, and well-founded fear of, US officers and citizens.

As we can see, therefore, the 'ticking bomb' justification of interrogational torture, as a 'one off' or as a limited practice, runs into a variety of difficulties. It relies on individuating actions and responsibilities in ways that don't map onto actual political situations; it assumes a much greater degree of epistemic certainty than is likely about the 'terrorist' and about the security services' capacity to recognize and act on the truth; it neglects the unintended consequences of violent action. Over and above all this, however, the 'ticking terrorist bomb' scenario, like the consequentialist and the rights- and duty-based justifications discussed in chapter 2, treats torture as an instrument subservient to higher purposes. The meaning of torture is subsumed within the category of self-defence of the state against its enemies, or the defence of innocent victims against a culpable aggressor, or the rescue of the vulnerable from terrible harm or death. The meaning and effects of the practice of torture itself are bracketed off. This means that we do not have to think about how it is that the torturer is able to torture. What are their attitudes and skills? What kinds of beliefs about those they are going to hurt do they need to subscribe to? How do they control their own reactions to the wounds and the screams? From the point of view of its victims and of its perpetrators, we know that both are transformed and disabled by the infliction and suffering of torture. For them, neither the scene of torture nor its conditions and after-effects could be meaningfully described in terms of rescue or defence.

Anti-colonialism

Like state violence, justification of anti-colonial violence has been approached in consequentialist terms. In order to achieve justified liberation, as a last resort, armed struggle is justifiable as a means. Fanon's exhortation to African leaders and activists not to rule violence out can be read in this frame. However, in his sustained analysis of the dynamics of colonial and anti-colonial violence, Fanon emphasized above all the absence of choice facing those who fight colonialism. Even those in favour of non-violence must engage with the violence of colonialism. Colonialism itself is an absolute violence, and whatever is done to contest it cannot be external to, independent of, that violence. In such a context, to pretend to non-violence is hypocritical, as well as serving the interests of the colonial and native elites who have a joint interest in dividing the spoils between them in the process of decolonization.

Fanon identifies violence at all levels, and in all dimensions, of colonial society – from the existential, to the spatial and economic, as well as the legal and political constitution of colonial life. Violence is manifest not only in the continuous physical abuse of colonized peoples, but also in the racist categories through which they were defined, in the management of the spaces they could or could not enter, in their poverty and exploitation, and in the denial of their rights and citizenship. In this context, violence is the only route to liberation. But rather than its being figured as a lamentable means to a desirable end, it can be recouped as in and of itself a form of liberation. By acting violently, and engaging in action against oppressors, oppressed people could come to experience themselves as agents of historical transformation. This violence of the oppressed can be clearly distinguished from the violence of the oppressor. In contrast to the brutal, poisonous and destructive violence of colonialism, the anti-colonial fighter's violence is disciplined, healthy and constructive. The military organization of anti-colonial violence prefigures the post-colonial order with its authentic forms of organization and its care for the people. As we saw in chapter 3, the anti-colonial Algerian struggle escalated to war. This identification of revolution as war figured the FLN as a military body. Fanon admired its internal organization, while the identification of it as an army involved the endorsement of a manichaean distinction between the two sides of the battle. Out of this binary struggle against evil a new humanity can emerge.

This idealization of anti-colonial, disciplined and properly humanitarian violence, though, is in tension with Fanon's attention to political violence as practice and as experience. The distinction between good anti-colonial and bad colonial violence, and the vision of the liberated future that will be generated by anti-colonial violence, sit uncomfortably with his reports, as a practising psychiatrist, of the effects of violence. For both perpetrators and victims, violence has catastrophic psychological, emotional, social and physical effects. It lives on in individual dissociation, neurosis and psychosis, and in social and kin relations which are disordered and damaged.

The political and existential promise of violence – theorized and imagined as strategic gains, the forging of new powerful subjectivities, the building of institutions, the life of virtue, and the capacity for creativity – is confronted by the diminutions, subtractions and disablements of violence's bodily and psychic traces and echoes. Furthermore, as Fanon himself notes, a key enabling factor in the use of violence for revolution is an adaptation of the manichaean context of colonialism. As we noted in chapter 4, practices, actions and cultures of violence instantiate political hierarchy and exclusion, often legitimated ideologically through binary racialized and gendered distinctions about who counts as 'us' and who as 'them'. In both cases the figure drawn with the greatest contempt, and most deserving violent eradication, is that of the collaborator, the fellow traveller or compromiser. The violence of the colonizer and that of the colonized, from this point of view after the fact, seem much more similar than different, and they both cast a very long shadow over the post-colonial future.

Anti-capitalism

Ambivalence about violence is anchored in anarchism's rejection of pure instrumentalism in political action. Unlike marxist revolutionaries, anarchists are positioned against the idea that revolutionary classes and societies could utilize instruments of dictatorship as a stage on the way to revolutionary change. Instead, anarchists insist that the kinds of political relations they are aiming for should be reflected in the political practices through which they fight for their cause. Violence poses a problem. The question of whether it could, as a practice, be compatible with anarchist values comes into relation with the simultaneous question of whether, given the violence of capitalist states, and the war relations between capitalist classes and the people they oppress and exploit, it could possibly be avoided.

As mentioned in chapter 2, there has recently been a debate within anarchist anti-globalization and anti-militarism movements about so-called 'diversity of tactics'. Within this debate thinkers and activists seek to justify, or question the justification of, the use of different types and degrees of violence. Violence against property, intimidatory and exemplary vivid assertions of potentially violent and threatening energy (for example, blocs of activists running together), defensive or offensive engagement with police and security officers, and how these combine with other non-violent tactics are all discussed. Consequentialist arguments focus on the extent to which violence works. Rights-based arguments focus on the right of self-defence, and the obligation to defend oppressed and exploited people collectively from the predations of state and capital. Arguments from necessity emphasize that the society is maintained by violence; that non-violent political action is impossible in states which are policed and secured as capitalist states are, so the idea of non-violent political action, in any kind of confrontation with or challenge to state authority and economic power, is fanciful. Critically, the broader struggle against state and capitalism, and the clashes between anti-capitalist protestors and state officers, are conceptualized as war.

Some anti-capitalist anarchists, such as Peter Gelderloos in *The Failure of Nonviolence* (2015), make an instrumentalist case for 'diversity of tactics', on the grounds that violence works, whereas non-violence invariably concedes authority and power to the status quo, undermining the possibilities of change. Gelderloos also emphasizes the right of self-defence. His argument hinges on two distinct lines of reason. First, he argues that anarchist and other proponents of non-violence make the error of understanding violence as an overarching strategy, which impacts on political goals. Instead, it should be seen as a particular, local, time-specific tactic. Furthermore, a proper understanding of strategies and goals will not see these as in fixed relation to one another. By limiting the range of tactics available, non-violent protestors allow the authorities to police, to contain and hence to neutralize resistance. In some cases, protest organizers even actively carry out this neutralization, by taking police functions on themselves. Second, he problematizes the distinction between violence and non-violence. So-called non-violent organizers inevitably have to use degrees of what can only be called violence against demonstrators who dissent from their rules and standards of propriety. The violence of the non-violent is more than a paradox – it effectively colludes with the violence of the state. Police action at protests is the tip of a deep iceberg of violent relationships which can be presented as civility, reasonableness and normal (non-violent) politics. The contrary identification of politics with war legitimates a manichaean, zero-sum approach to conflict.

It also accesses discourses of war in which, traditionally, it has been possible to discriminate between the good violence and the bad, both in the process of engaging in war and in the course of war. A section of protestors in the anti-globalization action in Hamburg, at the 2017 G20 meeting, adopted a diversity of tactics. For those protestors using violence, destruction of property could be justified in relation to the wrongs of structural violence. Stores of global brands, or branches of banks, are manifestations of this violence. Attacks on police were justified in terms of self-defence, or of the ongoing war with the state. But this clear distinction between the good, constructive, justified violence of protest and the bad, oppressive, unjust violence of capital and state is difficult to hold. Many of those involved in the protests were highly ambivalent in their evaluations of the justified nature, or otherwise, of protestors' violence. In particular, violence did not stay within the bounds of attacks on clear manifestations of structural violence, nor were all targets obviously legitimate because they could be identified as the enemy in the war. Violence leaks, is liable to be misdirected, and comes to pervade the relationships between those who, ostensibly, are on the same side.

Disputes about uses of violence in anti-capitalist politics allow us to show some of the difficulties with the philosophical and political enterprise of justifying political violence. Consequentialist and rights-based arguments, used prospectively, rely on confidence that intended outcomes will be delivered. They also rely on analogies between protestors and innocent victims of imminent or actual harm from aggressors; and on the analogy of political conflict with war. These analogies have to be reinforced by arguments from necessity: violence is argued to be endemic to the capitalist order, both in the form of structural violence and in the form of the direct violence of state security forces. In such a context non-violence can only permit and license violence – so there can be no principled commitment to non-violent tactics. This means that violence is inevitable. So the problem is to ensure that the violence employed, the violence that prevails, is good as opposed to bad, less as opposed to more. In the arguments of activists like Gelderloos, terms such as 'courage' or 'creative' are attached to the violence that is to be endorsed. The violence that is condemned is brutal, and destructive.

In such accounts, as in other justificatory discourses, the experience and practice of violence are bracketed out. Violence is treated as if it could be deployed as a self-contained tool, and no account is taken of its broader and longer-lasting conditions and effects. In protests like those in Hamburg, horizontal political relations, between the individuals and groups who make up the wide and loose coalitional network of actors who aim in concert to challenge state and global capitalism, disappear and are replaced by a series of hierarchies. Paramilitary identities and styles both enact and symbolize the hierarchical separation of the warrior class from the rest. The identification of political protest with war means that the only positions possible are those of conquest or defeat. The solidarity among the bands of warriors, the exhilaration of the use of violence, are parasitic on relations of hierarchy and exclusion. This is both in relation to those against whom one fights, and also in relation to those who do not fight. The tension with anarchism's, and socialism's, orientation to horizontal political relations is clear. So is that with anarchism's principled rejection of instrumentalist means–ends thinking.

Conclusion

In this chapter we have looked at justifications of state and non-state political violence in the light of insights gained from previous chapters. It should be clear that we see profound problems with the ways in which interrogational torture, violent anti-colonial revolt and violent anti-capitalist revolution have most often been justified. In this respect, we keep coming back to certain points in support of our critique.

First, consequentialist (which could include purely strategic as well as moral) and rights-based justifications of political violence are bound up with questionable assumptions about the nature of political action. These are about knowledge, control and the instrumentality of violence. A variety of analogies between the actions and aims of various institutional and collective actors and scenarios of individual self-defence, punishment, rescue and war are also assumed to be cogent. Second, discriminations between good and bad violence are more difficult to stabilize and uphold than thinkers such as Machiavelli or Weber admit, or than Merleau-Ponty, Beauvoir or Fanon are able to establish convincingly. Third, justificatory arguments, whether invoking support from consequences, rights, virtue, aesthetics or creativity, all rely on the possibility of treating violence as individuated, as a specific countable episode that is open to judgement. We are assumed to be able to discriminate between the violence (which is bracketed out) and the foregrounded context that supposedly renders that violence acceptable.

This brings us to two further points made in this chapter. In the light of all these difficulties in discriminating between different manifestations of political violence, our argument is that we must take the practice of inflicting violence itself as the key to the meaning of violent action. Fourth, then, the justificatory strategies are not so easily distinguished from the actions they are called upon to justify. Rather, they are part of the enabling conditions for violence whether it is figured as self-defence, punishment, rescue or war. In other words, doing war and torture requires that we can think of doing war and torture as right. This in turn requires not only established lists of criteria such as we may find in international or domestic legislation, but all the ideological and normative preconditions necessary to be confident that it is acceptable to kill and maim others. Fifth, paying attention to what the practice of political violence actually involves suggests that this is often patently at odds with the ends that the violence is supposed to serve. This may be the reason that action descriptions of political violence rarely dwell on the presuppositions and implications of violent practice itself.

For us, this means that our ethical and political attention should be on the world that violence instantiates, as opposed to the world it is supposed to produce. This is not, we will argue, to put forward a purist pacifism. The claim that political violence can never be justified does not mean that violence in politics is always (if ever) evaded, or that violence is always retrospectively condemned. Rather, we rest our case on the claim that the experience, intersubjective relations and effects of political violence qua violence are certainly pain, trauma, hierarchy and exclusion. Other kinds of experiences, intersubjective relations and effects that may sometimes be bound up with political violence, from the joy of battle to securing democracy, are neither guaranteed nor determinable in advance. In other words, the risks of political judgement when it comes to the use of violence must be taken from the position that, in committing to violence, political actors are committing to something that cannot be made right.

Conclusion: Political Violence Can Never Be Justified

In chapter 4, we showed how feminist analysis has unpacked the meaning of political violence as a practice. Feminist thought and action have engaged with political violence in the broadest sense: from domestic and sexual violence, to conflictual relations within and between political movements, through violence in war, to structural violence and the connections between all of these. In our view, there are two particular strengths of feminist analysis. First, it has paid attention to the phenomenology of violence, as experience and practice. Second, feminism has unpacked, and subjected to systematic critique, the virtue, aesthetic and analogy arguments that so often take up the slack for the shortcomings of purely instrumental or rights-generated justifications of political violence.

Feminist awareness of the gendering of violence

and its modes of justification has meant that for many feminist thinkers and activists the question of violence is a conundrum. The project of feminist pacifism, and the commitment to challenging gendered violence with reconstructive feminist social and political relations, intersect with scepticism about the instrumentality- and necessity-style arguments we have analysed. But, for some feminist activists in particular, the imperative to self-defence against domestic and sexual violence has become the primary instance of justifiable political violence from a feminist point of view. The problem is that practices of political violence trade on and reproduce gendered relations of domination, but so too does entrenched structural violence. If non-violent politics ends up colluding with structural violence, and generating more subjective violence, feminist theory is caught in the recognisable conflict that generates the question 'Can political violence ever be justified?'

Our argument is that there is a way of answering that question, which builds on significant strands of feminist thinking. It rejects war and is oriented to non-violence. It takes seriously the view that politics proper, ideal politics, is threatened fundamentally by structures and practices of violence. It draws from the kind of phenomenological analysis of the meanings and experiences of violence that we have met in feminist argument and in the work of Fanon and Scarry. It is an answer that is very unlikely to satisfy anyone who subsumes politically violent action under any other action description – whether this be self-defence or defence of another, rescue of threatened innocents, the bringing about of a better world or the manifestation of virtues. Our answer denies any possibility that political violence can be justified. It denies this possibility as a political – not a moral, or an epistemic – judgement. It acknowledges the fact that any political judgement, including this one, carries the risk of violence within it, as does the political practice of non-violence that follows from this judgement. In other words, non-violence cannot guarantee the outcomes of action any more than can violence. But, as Gandhi argued in *'Hind Swaraj' and Other Writings* (1909), even if non-violence is a mistake, or the outcomes of non-violence do not match our intentions, it has two major advantages over violence. First, the practice of non-violence itself instantiates relations of respect, inclusion and being with others, as opposed to contempt and exclusion. Second, non-violence is much more likely to leave all political protagonists able to try again in case of failure, as opposed to tactics that will annihilate political opponents, yet are still likely to fail.

At the heart of our argument is rejection of any reduction of violence to an instrument for political action. We endorse the claim that violence itself, qua violence, is a practice and an experience that has a politics. This is essentially a politics of hierarchy and exclusion. Violence is not a tool for action separate from action; it builds edifices and structures of inequality, rejection and estrangement. We follow Arendt's argument that politics cannot be reducible to means–ends reasoning, but is about the construction of intersubjective worlds, in which no outcomes can be guaranteed. Violence constructs a world of hierarchical, zero-sum distinctions between warriors and non-warriors, between aggressors and victims. It simply is not like rescue, in which civil power acts in concert with civil need. It is somewhat like self-defence – to the extent that that is exemplified by a woman picking up a kitchen knife to fend off a beating. That complex action – the threat, the beating, the knife – destroys the world, reducing it to feeling and injury. If relationships are remade, in the context of attack and defence, they tend to be a remake of the very hierarchical, violence-ridden relationships that generated the violence in the first place. The violent action is not liberating. Liberation, if it comes, is only in deliberately quitting one set of relationships and entering into, building, another set. A non-violent power.

Precisely because this opposition to violence is a question of politics, the meaning and outcomes of non-violent power are no more guaranteed than those of violence. Retrospective judgements of politically violent action may always be different from prospective ones. But it is dangerous to use a language of justification here. The idea of justification is that it makes something right. This mistakenly implies that the politics of violence is capable of being defused or controlled. The language of justification is also fundamentally permissive. It establishes thresholds for action. Thus it is part of gendering and racializing discourses that make political violence a practice in which it is not only possible, but rather easy, to engage, providing that participants are trained, and entrained, to embody the appropriate ideologies, skills, propensities and habits.

The justifications we engaged with in chapter 2 relied on the possibility of separating not only violence, but also the practice of justification, from politics. The arguments we examined in chapter 3, in spite of their recognition of the immanent relation between violence and politics, sought to find alternative ethical or aesthetic criteria – beyond politics – through which judgements about better and worse, more or less, violence might be attained. The structuralist arguments of chapter 4 challenge such distinctions between violence and politics by stretching the concept of political violence to encompass all constraint, all distributional systems. But it is the achievement of feminist analysis in particular to have shown how modes of justification themselves are complicit with the conditions that enable political violence to flourish. We cannot justify political violence because we cannot, by any means, justify the conditions that are necessary for political violence to be possible. These are conditions for producing subjects who will find it acceptable to reduce others – the enemy, the foreigner, the ruling class, the colonized, the colonizer, the racialized and feminized subject – to nothing.

Sources and Further Reading

Works and thinkers discussed

Arendt, Hannah. (1951) *The Origins of Totalitarianism*, San Diego: Harcourt.

Arendt, Hannah. (1958) *The Human Condition*, Chicago: University of Chicago Press.

Arendt, Hannah. (1969) *On Violence*, New York: Harcourt Brace.

Beauvoir, Simone de. (1948) *The Ethics of Ambiguity*, New York: Citadel Press.

Bourdieu, Pierre. (1990 [1980]) *The Logic of Practice*, trans. Nice, Richard, Cambridge: Polity.

Bourdieu, Pierre. (1991 [1982]) *Language and Symbolic Power*, trans. Raymond, Gino and Adamson, Matthew, Cambridge: Polity.

Bourdieu, Pierre. (2001 [1988]) *Masculine Domination*, trans. Nice, Richard, Cambridge: Polity.

Fanon, Frantz. (1965 [1961]) *The Wretched of the Earth*, London: Penguin.

Fanon, Frantz. (1970 [1952]) *Black Skin, White Mask*, London: Paladin.

Filmer, Robert. (1991 [1680]) Patriarcha. In: Sommerville, Johann P. (ed.), *Filmer: Patriarcha and Other Writings*, Cambridge: Cambridge University Press, 1–68.

Galtung, Johan. (1975) *Essays in Peace Research*, Copenhagen: Ejlers.

Galtung, Johan. (1990) 'Cultural Violence', *Journal of Peace Research* 27 (3): 291–305.

Gandhi, Mohandas. (2009 [1909]) *'Hind Swaraj' and Other Writings*, ed. Parel, Anthony J., Cambridge: Cambridge University Press.

Gelderloos, Peter. (2007) *How Nonviolence Protects the State*, Cambridge, MA: South End Press.

Gelderloos, Peter. (2015) *The Failure of Nonviolence*, Seattle: Left Bank Books.

Hobbes, Thomas. (1996 [1651]) *Leviathan*, Oxford: Oxford University Press.

Honderich, Ted. (1977) *Three Essays on Political Violence*, Oxford: Blackwell.

Honderich, Ted. (2003) *Terrorism for Humanity: Inquiries in Political Philosophy*, London: Pluto Press.

Honderich, Ted. (2015 [1980]) *Violence for Equality: Inquiries in Political Philosophy*, New York: Routledge.

Kant, Immanuel. (1981 [1785]) *Grounding for the Metaphysics of Morals*, Indianapolis: Hackett.

Kant, Immanuel. (1991) *Political Writings*, Cambridge: Cambridge University Press.

Koestler, Arthur. (2005 [1940]) *Darkness at Noon*, London: Vintage Books.

Locke, John. (1960 [1690]) *Two Treatises of Government*, Cambridge: Cambridge University Press.

Machiavelli, Niccolò. (1961 [1532]) *The Prince*, Harmondsworth: Penguin.

Marx, Karl and Engels, Friedrich. (1977 [1848]) *Manifesto of the Communist Party*, Moscow: Progress.

Merleau-Ponty, Maurice. (1969 [1947]) *Humanism and Terror: An Essay on the Communist Problem*, Boston: Beacon Press.

Rawls, John. (1971) *A Theory of Justice*, Cambridge, MA: Harvard University Press.

Sartre, Jean-Paul. (2007) *Existentialism and Humanism*, London: Methuen.

Scarry, Elaine. (1985) *The Body in Pain: The Making and Unmaking of the World*, Oxford: Oxford University Press.

Sorel, Georges. (1999 [1908]) *Reflections on Violence*, Cambridge: Cambridge University Press.

Tolstoy, Leo. (1894) *The Kingdom of God is Within You, or: Christianity not as a Mystical Doctrine but as a New Conception of Life*, London: William Heinemann.

Weber, Max. (1978 [1921]) *Economy and Society*, 2

vols, eds. Roth, Guenther and Wittich, Claus, Berkeley: University of California Press.
Žižek, Slavoj. (2008) *Violence: Six Sideways Reflections*, London: Profile Books.

Further reading on cases discussed

These are listed in chronological order of the cases.

English civil wars and revolutions

Pincus, Steven. (2009) *1688: The First Modern Revolution*, New Haven: Yale University Press.

French revolution

Doyle, William. (2018 [1990]) *The Oxford History of the French Revolution*, Oxford: Oxford University Press.

Stalinist purges

Conquest, Robert. (2008 [1990]) *The Great Terror: A Reassessment*, Oxford: Oxford University Press.

German resistance

Mommsen, Hans. (2003) *Alternatives to Hitler: German Resistance Under the Third Reich*, Princeton: Princeton University Press.

Algerian war

Horne, Alistair. (2012 [1977]) *A Savage War of Peace: Algeria 1954–1962*, London: Pan.

Macey, David. (2000) *Frantz Fanon: A Life*, London: Granta Books.

Northern Ireland Troubles

McKittrick, David and McVea, David. (2012) *Making Sense of the Troubles: A History of the Northern Ireland Conflict*, London: Viking Press.

Italian 'years of lead'

Della Porta, Donatella. (1995) *Social Movements, Political Violence, and the State: A Comparative Analysis of Italy and Germany*, Cambridge: Cambridge University Press.

Della Porta, Donatella. (2013) *Clandestine Political Violence*, Cambridge: Cambridge University Press.

Moss, David. (1989) *The Politics of Left-Wing Violence in Italy 1969–1985*, Basingstoke: Macmillan.

Anti-capitalist actions

Gordon, Uri. (2008) *Anarchy Alive: Anti-Authoritarian Politics from Practice to Theory*, London: Pluto Press.

Graeber, David. (2009) *Direct Action: An Ethnography*, Oakland: AK Press.

State torture of terrorists

Greenberg, Karen J. and Dratel, Joshua L. (2005) *The Torture Papers: The Road to Abu Ghraib*, Cambridge: Cambridge University Press.

Electoral violence

Söderberg Kovacs, Mimmi and Bjarnesen, Jesper (eds.). (2018) *Violence in African Elections: Between Democracy and Big Man Politics*, London: Zed Books.

Further reading on violence, politics and justification

Balibar, Etienne. (2015) *Violence and Civility: On the Limits of Political Philosophy*, New York: Columbia University Press.

Basham, Victoria. (2013) *War, Identity and the Liberal State: Everyday Experiences of the Geopolitical in the Armed Forces*, Abingdon: Routledge.

Bernstein, Richard. (2013) *Violence: Thinking without Banisters*, Cambridge: Polity.

Bufacchi, Vittorio. (2007) *Violence and Social Justice*, Basingstoke: Palgrave Macmillan.

Butler, Judith. (2004) *Precarious Life: The Powers of Mourning and Violence*, London: Verso.

Butler, Judith. (2009) *Frames of War: When Is Life Grievable?*, London: Verso.

Card, Claudia. (2010) *Confronting Evils: Terrorism, Torture, Genocide*, Cambridge: Cambridge University Press.

Cavarero, Adriana. (2011 [2007]) *Horrorism: Naming Contemporary Violence*, New York: Columbia University Press.

Chenoweth, Erica and Stephan, Maria J. (2011) *Why Civil Resistance Works: The Strategic Logic of Nonviolent Conflict*, New York: Columbia University Press.

Coady, C. A. J. (2008) *Morality and Political Violence*, Cambridge: Cambridge University Press.

Collins, Randall. (2008) *Violence: A Micro-Sociological Theory*, Princeton: Princeton University Press.

Corrigan, Paul and Sayer, Derek. (1985) *The Great Arch: English State Formation as Cultural Revolution*, Oxford: Blackwell.

Critchley, Simon. (2012) *Infinitely Demanding: Ethics of Commitment, Politics of Resistance*, London: Verso.

Duriesmith, David. (2017) *Masculinity and New War: The Gendered Dynamics of Contemporary Armed Conflict*, Abingdon: Routledge.

Finlay, Christopher. (2015) *Terrorism and the Right to Resist*, Cambridge: Cambridge University Press.

Frazer, Elizabeth and Hutchings, Kimberly. (2007) 'Argument and Rhetoric in the Justification of Political Violence', *European Journal of Political Theory* 6 (2): 180–99.

Frazer, Elizabeth and Hutchings, Kimberly. (2008) 'On Politics and Violence: Arendt contra Fanon', *Contemporary Political Theory* 7 (1): 90–108.

Frazer, Elizabeth and Hutchings, Kimberly. (2016) 'Anarchist Ambivalence: Politics and Violence in the Thought of Bakunin, Tolstoy and Kropotkin', *European Journal of Political Theory*, 10 March.

Ginbar, Yuval. (2008) *Why Not Torture Terrorists? Moral, Practical and Legal Aspects of the Ticking Bomb Justification for Torture*, Oxford: Oxford University Press.

Hewlett, Nick. (2016) *Blood and Progress: Violence in Pursuit of Emancipation*, Edinburgh: Edinburgh University Press.

Kalyvas, Stathis. (2006) *The Logic of Violence in Civil War*, Cambridge: Cambridge University Press.

Kinsella, Helen. (2011) *The Image Before the Weapon: A Critical History of the Distinction between Combatant and Civilian*. Ithaca: Cornell University Press.

Levinson, Sanford (ed.). (2004) *Torture: A Collection*, Oxford: Oxford University Press.

Marshall, Peter. (2007) *Demanding the Impossible*, London: William Collins.

McMahan, Jeff. (2009) *Killing in War*, Oxford: Clarendon Press.

Ruddick, Sara. (1989) *Maternal Thinking: Towards a Politics of Peace*, Boston: Beacon Press.

Sjoberg, Laura. (2013) *Gendering Global Conflict: Towards a Feminist Theory of War*, New York: Columbia University Press.

Steinhoff, Uti. (2007) *On the Ethics of War and Terrorism*, Oxford: Oxford University Press.

Tilly, Charles and Tarrow, Sidney. (2015) *Contentious Politics*, 2nd edn, Oxford: Oxford University Press.